Introduction to IT Service Management (ITSM) Frameworks

James Relington

DEDICATION

To those who seek knowledge, inspiration, and new perspectives—
may this book be a companion on your journey, a spark for curiosity,
and a reminder that every page turned is a step toward discovery.

AKNOWLEDGEMENTS

I would like to express my deepest gratitude to everyone who contributed to the creation of this book. To my colleagues and mentors, your insights and expertise have been invaluable. A special thank you to my family and friends for their unwavering support and encouragement throughout this journey.

The Evolution of IT Service Management

IT Service Management (ITSM) has undergone significant transformation over the decades, shaped by advances in technology, evolving business needs, and changing perceptions of IT's role within organizations. In the early days of computing, IT was primarily viewed as a support function, an isolated department focused on maintaining hardware and software infrastructure. IT departments were tasked with keeping systems running smoothly, often with little involvement in the overall business strategy. As organizations began to recognize the strategic value of IT, the approach to managing IT services evolved. This shift marked the beginning of a new era for ITSM, one that would emphasize customer satisfaction, service delivery, and continuous improvement.

In the 1980s and early 1990s, IT service management was often informal and reactive. IT departments operated in silos, and their primary concern was keeping systems operational. There was little attention paid to the customer experience or to aligning IT services with business objectives. As the complexity of IT systems grew, organizations began to realize that a more structured and systematic approach was needed to manage IT services effectively. This realization led to the development of early ITSM frameworks and methodologies, which sought to address these challenges.

The introduction of the Information Technology Infrastructure Library (ITIL) in the late 1980s was a turning point for ITSM. ITIL was created by the British government's Central Computer and Telecommunications Agency (CCTA) as a set of best practices for IT management. Its goal was to provide a comprehensive framework for managing IT services, ensuring that IT departments could deliver high-quality, reliable services to meet business needs. ITIL emphasized the importance of service management processes, such as incident management, change management, and service desk support, and promoted a holistic approach to managing IT services throughout their lifecycle.

As ITIL gained traction, organizations began to recognize the value of implementing structured processes to improve service delivery and reduce costs. In the 1990s, ITSM frameworks began to gain wider acceptance, and organizations began to adopt ITIL to standardize their IT service management practices. ITIL provided a common language and framework for IT departments to follow, helping to bridge the gap between IT operations and business goals. This period also saw the rise of service-level agreements (SLAs), which defined the expectations for service performance and availability between IT departments and their customers.

Throughout the late 1990s and early 2000s, the role of IT in business continued to evolve. The growth of the internet, the rise of e-commerce, and the increasing reliance on technology for critical business functions led to a fundamental shift in how IT services were viewed. IT was no longer seen as a support function but as a core enabler of business success. As a result, ITSM frameworks began to place greater emphasis on aligning IT services with business objectives. Organizations sought to deliver services that not only met technical requirements but also contributed to business outcomes, such as improved customer satisfaction, increased efficiency, and enhanced competitiveness.

During this period, the focus of ITSM expanded beyond infrastructure management to include service delivery, customer experience, and continuous improvement. The introduction of concepts such as Total Quality Management (TQM) and Six Sigma into the ITSM world helped organizations adopt a more proactive approach to service management. IT departments began to focus on identifying and eliminating inefficiencies in their processes, improving the quality of service delivery, and ensuring that services met or exceeded customer expectations.

In the 2010s, ITSM frameworks continued to evolve, influenced by the rise of cloud computing, agile methodologies, and DevOps practices. The traditional, rigid approach to ITSM was increasingly seen as incompatible with the fast-paced, dynamic nature of modern business environments. Organizations began to adopt more flexible, iterative approaches to service management, allowing them to respond more quickly to changing business needs and technological advancements. This shift was particularly evident in the rise of agile ITSM, which emphasized collaboration, flexibility, and continuous delivery of value.

The rise of cloud computing also had a significant impact on ITSM. With the proliferation of cloud-based services, IT departments were no longer solely responsible for managing physical infrastructure. Instead, they were tasked with managing a mix of on-premise and cloud-based services, which required new approaches to service management. ITSM frameworks evolved to accommodate this shift, with a greater emphasis on managing third-party providers, ensuring service continuity across hybrid environments, and integrating cloud-based services into existing ITSM processes.

Another key development in ITSM during this time was the growing importance of automation. With the increasing complexity of IT systems and the need for rapid response times, organizations began to embrace automation as a way to improve efficiency, reduce errors, and streamline service delivery. Automation tools were integrated into ITSM processes, such as incident management, change management, and problem management, enabling organizations to handle a higher volume of requests and incidents with greater speed and accuracy. This also allowed IT departments to focus on more strategic tasks, such as improving service quality and aligning IT services with business goals.

As we move into the 2020s, ITSM continues to evolve, driven by new technological advancements and the changing expectations of businesses and customers. The rise of artificial intelligence (AI) and machine learning is expected to have a transformative impact on ITSM, enabling organizations to leverage data analytics and predictive insights to optimize service delivery and proactively address issues before they arise. The integration of AI into ITSM processes will enable greater automation, more accurate incident resolution, and improved customer experiences.

The increasing focus on customer-centric ITSM is another key trend shaping the future of the field. Organizations are recognizing that IT services must be aligned not only with business goals but also with the needs and expectations of end-users. The customer experience has become a critical metric for success, and IT departments are working to improve user satisfaction through personalized services, self-service portals, and proactive support. ITSM is no longer just about managing technology; it is about delivering value to customers and ensuring that IT services contribute to the overall success of the business.

The evolution of ITSM has been shaped by numerous factors, from technological advancements to changes in organizational priorities. What began as a set of best practices for managing IT services has transformed into a comprehensive, dynamic approach to service management that is critical to the success of modern organizations. As technology continues to evolve, ITSM will undoubtedly continue to adapt, ensuring that IT services remain aligned with business needs and deliver value to both organizations and their customers.

Defining IT Service Management

IT Service Management (ITSM) is a set of practices, processes, and policies designed to ensure that information technology (IT) services are delivered in alignment with the needs and goals of an organization. The primary focus of ITSM is on the customer, ensuring that IT services are not only efficient and effective but also responsive to the evolving demands of the business and its stakeholders. Over the years, ITSM has become an essential aspect of organizational operations, as it helps businesses manage their IT infrastructure and services in a structured, consistent manner. Its purpose is to enhance service quality, minimize risks, reduce costs, and ultimately contribute to the success of the business.

The core of ITSM lies in the concept of services. In this context, a service is defined as a means of delivering value to customers by facilitating outcomes that the customer wants to achieve, without the customer having to manage specific costs and risks. Unlike traditional IT management, which often focused on the technical aspects of IT systems, ITSM places a stronger emphasis on the service itself, the experience of the user, and the value that service brings to the organization. IT services can range from basic infrastructure management, such as networks and servers, to more complex business services, such as customer relationship management (CRM) platforms and enterprise resource planning (ERP) systems.

One of the key principles of ITSM is the notion of the service lifecycle, which consists of a series of stages that an IT service goes through, from its initial planning and design to its eventual retirement. These stages include service strategy, service design, service transition, service operation, and continual service improvement. Each stage involves different activities and processes that contribute to the overall management of the service, ensuring that it is delivered efficiently, meets customer expectations, and evolves in line with business requirements. The service lifecycle framework emphasizes the need for ongoing evaluation and improvement to ensure that IT services remain relevant and valuable over time.

In order to manage IT services effectively, organizations need to establish a set of processes and practices that guide the way IT services are designed, delivered, and supported. These processes cover a wide range of activities, from incident management and change management to problem management, capacity planning, and security management. ITSM processes are designed to be repeatable, measurable, and consistent, ensuring that IT services are delivered with a high degree of reliability and quality. They are also designed to be flexible, allowing organizations to adapt to changing business needs and technological advancements. By defining clear processes for managing IT services, organizations can reduce the likelihood of service disruptions, enhance customer satisfaction, and improve the overall efficiency of their IT operations.

One of the foundational concepts in ITSM is the service level agreement (SLA). An SLA is a formal agreement between an IT service provider and its customers that defines the expected level of service, including aspects such as service availability, response times, and performance. SLAs serve as a key tool for managing customer expectations, as they clearly outline what customers can expect from the IT services they receive. They also serve as a basis for measuring service performance, allowing both the service provider and the customer to assess whether the agreed-upon service levels are being met. By defining and managing SLAs, organizations can ensure that their IT services align with customer expectations and business needs.

Another important aspect of ITSM is the role of the service desk. The service desk is the primary point of contact between IT and its customers, responsible for managing service requests, incidents, and queries. It plays a crucial role in ensuring that IT services are delivered efficiently and effectively, as it helps to resolve issues, provide support, and coordinate service delivery across different teams and departments. The service desk is also responsible for collecting and analyzing data related to service performance, customer satisfaction, and service improvement opportunities. This information is invaluable for identifying trends, addressing recurring issues, and ensuring that IT services continue to meet the needs of the business.

In recent years, the field of ITSM has been influenced by several key trends, including the rise of cloud computing, agile methodologies, and DevOps practices. Cloud computing has transformed the way IT services are delivered, enabling organizations to access and consume IT resources on-demand, without the need to manage physical infrastructure. As a result, ITSM practices have evolved to accommodate the complexities of managing hybrid environments that include both on-premise and cloud-based services. This has led to the development of new ITSM frameworks and tools designed to support cloud service management, including service catalog management, cloud security, and cloud performance monitoring.

Agile methodologies and DevOps practices have also had a significant impact on ITSM. Agile emphasizes collaboration, flexibility, and rapid delivery of value, which has led organizations to adopt more iterative and incremental approaches to service management. DevOps, which focuses on breaking down the traditional silos between development and operations teams, has encouraged a more integrated approach to

ITSM, where IT service delivery is closely aligned with software development and deployment processes. These trends have resulted in a shift towards more dynamic, customer-centric ITSM practices that are better able to respond to the fast-paced nature of modern business environments.

Despite these changes, the fundamental principles of ITSM remain consistent. ITSM is still fundamentally about delivering high-quality IT services that meet the needs of the business and its customers. However, the methods and tools used to achieve this goal have evolved, reflecting the growing complexity of IT systems, the increasing importance of technology in business, and the need for more flexible, responsive service delivery. As organizations continue to rely on technology to drive their operations, the importance of ITSM will only continue to grow. ITSM provides the framework necessary to manage IT services in a way that maximizes value for the organization, ensures the continuity of critical services, and supports the achievement of business objectives. In this sense, ITSM is not just a set of processes and practices; it is a critical enabler of business success, helping organizations leverage technology to drive innovation, improve efficiency, and enhance customer experiences.

Core Concepts of ITSM

The field of IT Service Management (ITSM) revolves around a set of core concepts that are designed to ensure the effective delivery, support, and management of IT services within an organization. These concepts form the foundation of ITSM practices, guiding organizations in their approach to delivering services that align with business objectives and meet customer expectations. The importance of these core concepts cannot be overstated, as they provide the structure and framework that organizations rely on to ensure the consistency, efficiency, and quality of their IT services.

At the heart of ITSM is the notion of a service. A service in ITSM is defined as a means of delivering value to customers by helping them achieve specific outcomes, without them having to manage the costs and risks associated with the delivery of the service. This is a shift away from the traditional view of IT, where the focus was primarily on technology and infrastructure. Instead, ITSM emphasizes the value of services, the customer experience, and the outcomes that these services deliver to the organization. The service itself is the key to ITSM, and everything within the framework of ITSM is designed to ensure that the service is delivered in a manner that meets both business and customer expectations.

A critical concept within ITSM is the service lifecycle. The service lifecycle describes the stages through which a service passes from inception to retirement. These stages include service strategy, service design, service transition, service operation, and continual service improvement. Each stage is interconnected and builds upon the previous one, ensuring that the service is not only delivered effectively but also continuously improved throughout its lifecycle. Service strategy involves understanding the business needs and defining the services that will deliver the most value. Service design focuses on the planning and designing of services to meet the defined business needs. Service transition involves the implementation and deployment of the services, while service operation ensures that services are delivered efficiently and effectively on a day-to-day basis. Continual service improvement is about assessing the service's performance, identifying areas for improvement, and ensuring that the service evolves in line with changing business requirements.

Another core concept of ITSM is the focus on processes. ITSM is built around a number of key processes that are designed to ensure that IT services are delivered in a structured and efficient manner. These processes are not just about technical implementation; they also consider the broader goals of the organization, including customer satisfaction, cost management, and alignment with business objectives. Common ITSM processes include incident management, problem management, change management, and service level management. Incident management focuses on restoring normal service operation as quickly as possible following an interruption, ensuring minimal disruption to the business. Problem management seeks to identify and resolve the root causes of incidents to prevent recurrence. Change management ensures that changes to IT systems are made in a controlled and predictable manner to minimize risk. Service level management is concerned with defining, negotiating, and managing service level agreements (SLAs) between IT service providers and their customers to ensure that services meet agreed-upon standards.

Service level agreements are a crucial part of the ITSM framework. An SLA is a formal agreement between the IT service provider and the customer that defines the expected level of service. This includes metrics such as service availability, response times, and performance standards. SLAs help to manage customer expectations by making clear the level of service that will be provided and serve as a baseline for measuring service performance. By establishing SLAs, IT organizations can ensure that they deliver services that meet the specific needs of the business, while also providing a framework for continuous improvement based on performance against the agreed standards.

The concept of customer-centricity is also deeply embedded within ITSM. In traditional IT management, the focus was often on maintaining systems and infrastructure, with little regard for the customer experience. However, with ITSM, the emphasis is placed on understanding and meeting customer needs. This means that IT departments must go beyond just delivering a service and instead focus on providing value to the customer. Customer-centricity in ITSM involves ensuring that services are designed, delivered, and supported in a way that meets or exceeds the expectations of the customer. This approach fosters better relationships between IT and the business, helping to align IT services with organizational goals and improve overall service quality.

The concept of continual service improvement (CSI) is another fundamental element of ITSM. CSI focuses on identifying areas for improvement in service delivery and making incremental changes that lead to better outcomes for the business and the customer. This concept is rooted in the idea that no service or process is ever perfect, and that there is always room for improvement. By constantly assessing performance, gathering feedback, and analyzing data, organizations can identify opportunities to enhance service quality, reduce costs, and increase efficiency. CSI is a key part of the service lifecycle, as it ensures that services evolve to meet changing business needs and technological advancements.

A related concept within ITSM is the idea of governance. ITSM frameworks provide a structure for ensuring that IT services are aligned with organizational goals and are managed in a way that supports business success. Governance in ITSM involves defining policies, standards, and procedures that ensure services are delivered in a consistent, efficient, and accountable manner. It also involves ensuring that IT services are compliant with relevant regulations, industry standards, and best practices. Effective governance is essential for managing risk, ensuring compliance, and achieving the desired outcomes from IT services.

The role of the service desk is another key concept in ITSM. The service desk acts as the primary point of contact between the IT department and the business. It serves as the hub for managing service requests, incidents, and other interactions with users. A well-functioning service desk is essential for the smooth operation of IT services, as it provides support for users, resolves issues quickly, and ensures that IT services are aligned with business needs. The service desk is also a valuable source of data, providing insights into common issues, trends, and areas for improvement. This information can be used to improve service delivery, enhance user satisfaction, and ensure that services continue to meet the evolving needs of the business.

Finally, the concept of integration is critical within ITSM. IT services rarely exist in isolation, and they must often be integrated with other systems, processes, and business functions. Integration in ITSM ensures that IT services are not just effective in isolation but also contribute to the broader goals of the organization. It enables seamless collaboration between different departments, ensures the smooth flow of information, and allows for better coordination of service delivery across the entire organization.

The core concepts of ITSM are fundamental to the successful management and delivery of IT services. These concepts ensure that IT services are not only efficient and cost-effective but also aligned with business objectives and customer expectations. By focusing on service delivery, processes, governance, continual improvement, and customer-centricity, ITSM helps organizations navigate the complexities of modern IT environments and deliver value through technology.

The Role of ITSM in Modern Organizations

In today's fast-paced, technology-driven world, organizations are increasingly dependent on IT to support their operations, drive innovation, and meet business objectives. As IT has become a core enabler of success across industries, the need for structured, effective management of IT services has never been more critical. IT Service Management (ITSM) plays a pivotal role in modern organizations by providing the framework and processes necessary to deliver high-quality IT services that are aligned with business needs and customer expectations. Its importance extends beyond just technical management, influencing business strategies, customer relationships, and overall organizational efficiency.

The role of ITSM in modern organizations begins with its focus on service delivery. In the past, IT departments were primarily concerned with maintaining the infrastructure and ensuring that systems remained operational. Today, however, ITSM emphasizes the delivery of services that provide value to the business and its customers. These services can range from basic IT support and infrastructure management to complex business-critical applications. ITSM enables organizations to take a more holistic approach to service delivery, ensuring that IT is not just a support function, but an integral part of the organization's success. By focusing on the quality, reliability, and consistency of IT services, ITSM ensures that technology is leveraged to drive business outcomes and enhance customer experiences.

One of the key aspects of ITSM in modern organizations is its alignment with business objectives. As businesses become increasingly digital and technology-driven, IT must be seen not only as a cost center but as a strategic asset that directly contributes to organizational goals. ITSM frameworks provide the tools and processes necessary to ensure that IT services are not only efficient but also in sync with the overall business strategy. For example, by implementing frameworks such as ITIL, organizations can define services that support business needs, ensure that they are delivered in a way that meets customer expectations, and establish clear metrics for service performance. This alignment between IT and business ensures that the organization can respond more effectively to changes in the market, enhance its competitive edge, and maintain its growth trajectory.

The increasing complexity of IT systems and the growing demand for faster, more flexible service delivery have made it essential for organizations to embrace a more agile approach to service management. In modern organizations, ITSM plays a central role in facilitating this shift. ITSM processes and practices are designed to be flexible and adaptable, allowing organizations to respond quickly to changing business needs, technological advancements, and market conditions. Whether through agile methodologies, cloud computing, or DevOps practices, ITSM provides the structure that organizations need to deliver services in a more dynamic, customer-centric way. By enabling faster delivery of services and more efficient handling of incidents, changes, and problems, ITSM helps organizations remain responsive and competitive in a rapidly evolving environment.

Furthermore, ITSM contributes to risk management within modern organizations. As organizations rely more heavily on technology, the risks associated with IT operations have also increased. From data breaches and cybersecurity threats to system failures and downtime, the potential for disruptions has never been higher. ITSM helps organizations mitigate these risks by providing processes for managing incidents, changes, and problems in a structured and controlled manner. For example, incident management processes ensure that disruptions to services are addressed quickly, minimizing the impact on the business. Change management processes ensure that changes to IT systems are made in a controlled manner, reducing the risk of errors or system failures. By providing a clear framework for managing IT operations, ITSM helps organizations identify potential risks, implement preventive measures, and maintain business continuity.

Another important role of ITSM in modern organizations is its focus on customer satisfaction. In a world where customer expectations are constantly evolving, organizations must ensure that they are delivering IT services that meet or exceed those expectations. ITSM processes such as service level management, incident management, and customer support are designed to ensure that services are delivered consistently, efficiently, and with a high level of quality. By managing customer expectations through service level agreements (SLAs), organizations can ensure that they are meeting agreed-upon performance standards and addressing issues promptly. The service desk, as the primary point of contact between IT and end-users, plays a critical role in maintaining customer satisfaction. By providing timely support and resolving issues efficiently, the service desk ensures that users have a positive experience with IT services, which in turn enhances the overall customer experience and strengthens the organization's reputation.

As the nature of IT services evolves, ITSM also plays a key role in driving continuous improvement. Modern organizations must be able to adapt to the ever-changing demands of their customers, competitors, and the market. ITSM frameworks are designed to facilitate ongoing evaluation and improvement of IT services, ensuring that they continue to meet business needs and customer expectations. Continual service improvement (CSI) is an integral part of ITSM, encouraging organizations to regularly assess their services, identify areas for improvement, and make incremental changes that lead to better outcomes. By embracing a culture of continual improvement, organizations can enhance the quality of their services, reduce costs, increase efficiency, and ensure that IT remains aligned with business goals.

In addition to service delivery, risk management, and customer satisfaction, ITSM also plays a critical role in fostering collaboration across different departments within the organization. As businesses become more reliant on technology, IT services often span multiple functions, from infrastructure and application management to customer support and business analytics. ITSM processes promote collaboration by providing a common framework for managing IT services across different teams and departments. For example, change management processes require coordination between development, operations, and other stakeholders to ensure that changes are made smoothly and without disrupting service delivery. Similarly, incident management processes often involve collaboration between IT teams, customer support, and business units to resolve issues quickly and efficiently. This cross-functional collaboration is essential for ensuring that IT services are delivered in a way that meets the needs of the business and its customers.

The role of ITSM in modern organizations is also closely tied to the growing trend of digital transformation. As organizations embrace new technologies such as cloud computing, artificial intelligence, and the Internet of Things (IoT), ITSM provides the framework for managing these complex systems and ensuring that they deliver value to the business. ITSM processes must be adaptable to accommodate the integration of new technologies, and ITSM frameworks are evolving to support the management of emerging technologies in ways that align with business goals. Digital transformation is fundamentally reshaping the way organizations operate, and ITSM plays a key role in ensuring that IT services are aligned with this transformation and continue to support the business as it evolves.

In summary, ITSM is essential to the success of modern organizations. It provides the structure, processes, and practices necessary to deliver high-quality IT services that are aligned with business objectives and meet customer expectations. By focusing on service delivery, business alignment, risk management, customer satisfaction, continuous improvement, and collaboration, ITSM enables organizations to leverage technology to drive business success. As the role of IT continues to expand in the digital age, the importance of ITSM will only continue to grow, helping organizations to adapt, innovate, and stay competitive in an increasingly technology-driven world.

The Importance of Service Lifecycle Management

Service Lifecycle Management (SLM) is a fundamental aspect of IT Service Management (ITSM), offering a structured approach to the management of IT services from their initial conception through to their retirement. The concept of lifecycle management emphasizes that IT services should not be viewed in isolation but as part of an ongoing process that spans multiple stages, each of which plays a critical role in ensuring that services are effective, efficient, and aligned with business goals. The importance of Service Lifecycle Management lies in its ability to guide organizations in creating, maintaining, and improving IT services that consistently meet the needs of both the business and its customers.

The service lifecycle begins with the service strategy phase, where the goals and objectives of the service are defined, and continues through design, transition, operation, and continual improvement. Each phase of the lifecycle is interconnected, with the outcome of one stage influencing the success of the next. For example, the strategic planning of a service during the service strategy phase directly impacts its design, transition, and operational phases. Without a structured lifecycle approach, organizations risk creating services that fail to align with business needs or deliver the expected value to customers. By ensuring that each phase is properly managed, organizations can optimize service quality, minimize risks, and maximize the return on investment for IT services.

One of the key reasons Service Lifecycle Management is so critical is its focus on ensuring that services are consistently aligned with the evolving needs of the business. In a rapidly changing business environment, organizations must be agile and responsive to market shifts, technological advancements, and changing customer expectations. SLM provides the framework necessary to make sure that IT services are designed and delivered in a way that supports these changes. During the service strategy phase, organizations assess business requirements and market conditions, which informs the design of services that can meet those needs both now and in the future. The lifecycle approach ensures that services remain flexible and adaptable to changing circumstances, making it easier for organizations to adjust to new challenges or opportunities.

The service design phase is another critical component of Service Lifecycle Management, as it focuses on translating business requirements into well-defined and actionable service designs. A well-structured service design process ensures that services are created with the right resources, capabilities, and technologies in place. It involves designing services that are not only technically sound but also customer-centric, ensuring that they deliver value to the business and meet user expectations. This phase includes the creation of service catalogs, which outline the available services and their characteristics, and service level agreements (SLAs), which define the expected performance and availability of the services. By carefully planning the design of services, organizations can avoid the pitfalls of poorly designed services that fail to deliver on their promises or fail to meet customer needs.

Once a service has been designed, it enters the service transition phase, where it is implemented and deployed into the live environment. This phase is critical for ensuring that services are delivered smoothly and without disruption. Service transition involves coordinating various activities, including testing, deployment, and training, to ensure that the service is fully functional and ready for use. Effective transition management reduces the risk of service failure during deployment, ensuring that the service is stable and performs as expected when it goes live. The service transition phase also includes the management of any changes that may affect the service, ensuring that they are handled in a controlled and predictable manner. Without a structured service transition process, organizations risk introducing errors or issues into live systems, which can negatively impact service delivery and customer satisfaction.

The service operation phase focuses on the day-to-day management and delivery of IT services. During this phase, services are monitored and supported to ensure that they continue to meet business requirements and customer expectations. Service operation includes key processes such as incident management, problem management, and service desk support, all of which are designed to ensure that IT services are delivered efficiently and with minimal disruption. Effective service operation is essential for maintaining service quality and ensuring that issues are resolved quickly to minimize downtime and disruptions to business operations. The goal of service operation is to provide a stable, reliable service that enables the organization to meet its business objectives.

Continual service improvement (CSI) is the final stage in the Service Lifecycle Management process, focusing on the ongoing evaluation and improvement of IT services. CSI is based on the premise that no service is ever perfect and that there is always room for improvement. This phase involves regularly assessing service performance, gathering feedback from customers, and analyzing data to identify areas for improvement. By continuously monitoring and refining services, organizations can ensure that they remain relevant and effective in meeting the needs of the business and its customers. Continual improvement helps organizations stay competitive by enabling them to adapt to changing business environments, address emerging challenges, and deliver greater value to customers over time.

The benefits of Service Lifecycle Management are far-reaching. One of the primary benefits is the ability to manage risk more effectively. By carefully planning and managing each phase of the service lifecycle, organizations can identify potential risks early on and take proactive measures to mitigate them. For example, during the service design phase, risks related to scalability, performance, or security can be identified and addressed before the service is deployed. Similarly, during the service transition phase, proper testing and validation can help identify potential issues that may arise during deployment, allowing organizations to resolve them before the service is live. By proactively managing risks, organizations can avoid costly disruptions, minimize downtime, and ensure that services are delivered without unexpected failures.

Another key benefit of Service Lifecycle Management is the ability to improve service quality. By following a structured approach that encompasses planning, design, transition, operation, and continual improvement, organizations can ensure that services are of the highest quality throughout their lifecycle. Service quality is monitored at each stage, and improvements are made based on performance data and customer feedback. As a result, services become more efficient, reliable, and customer-friendly over time, which contributes to greater user satisfaction and improved business outcomes.

Service Lifecycle Management also helps organizations optimize their resources. By aligning services with business goals and customer needs, organizations can ensure that resources are allocated effectively and efficiently. This includes optimizing both human resources and technological resources, ensuring that the right people and tools are in place to deliver the best possible services. By reducing waste and improving resource utilization, organizations can lower costs and improve overall efficiency.

The structured approach of Service Lifecycle Management also facilitates better communication and collaboration across different teams and departments within the organization. Because SLM provides a common framework for service management, it encourages cross-functional collaboration between IT, business units, and customers. This collaborative approach ensures that all stakeholders are involved in the service management process, resulting in services that are more closely aligned with business needs and customer expectations.

In a modern, technology-driven business environment, the importance of Service Lifecycle Management cannot be overstated. It is a critical component of ITSM that ensures services are delivered in a way that maximizes value to the business while minimizing risks and inefficiencies. By carefully managing the entire lifecycle of IT services, organizations can enhance service quality, reduce costs, and improve customer satisfaction, all while staying agile and adaptable in a rapidly changing world.

ITSM Frameworks: An Overview

In the world of Information Technology Service Management (ITSM), frameworks play a vital role in shaping the way IT services are delivered, managed, and supported. These frameworks provide structured methodologies, best practices, and guidelines to organizations, helping them align their IT operations with business goals, improve service delivery, and ensure customer satisfaction. Over the years, several ITSM frameworks have emerged, each with its own focus, strengths, and areas of application. Understanding these frameworks and their relevance in modern organizations is essential for organizations aiming to optimize their IT services.

The primary function of an ITSM framework is to establish a standardized approach for managing IT services throughout their lifecycle. This includes everything from service strategy, design, and implementation, to operation and continual improvement. Frameworks provide a blueprint for organizations to follow, ensuring consistency and reliability in the delivery of IT services. By adopting an ITSM framework, organizations can reduce the risks associated with service delivery, enhance service quality, and ultimately deliver greater value to both the business and its customers.

One of the most widely recognized ITSM frameworks is the Information Technology Infrastructure Library, or ITIL. Developed in the 1980s by the British government, ITIL has evolved over time into the de facto standard for IT service management. ITIL provides a comprehensive set of best practices that cover all aspects of IT service management, from strategy and design to operation and continual improvement. It emphasizes the importance of aligning IT services with business objectives, focusing on customer satisfaction, and ensuring that IT services are delivered efficiently and effectively. ITIL's structured approach to service management has made it an essential tool for organizations looking to improve their IT operations and deliver high-quality services.

Another significant ITSM framework is the ISO/IEC 20000 standard, which provides a formal specification for establishing, implementing, and maintaining an effective ITSM system. Unlike ITIL, which is a collection of best practices, ISO/IEC 20000 is a certifiable standard that organizations can use to demonstrate their adherence to global ITSM best practices. The ISO/IEC 20000 standard provides a framework for organizations to develop an ITSM system that meets international standards for quality and service delivery. Achieving ISO/IEC 20000 certification signifies that an organization's IT service management processes are in line with industry standards and best practices, providing a competitive advantage and enhancing customer confidence.

While ITIL and ISO/IEC 20000 are among the most well-known ITSM frameworks, there are other frameworks that organizations may choose to adopt depending on their specific needs and objectives. One such framework is COBIT (Control Objectives for Information and Related Technologies), which is primarily focused on IT governance, risk management, and compliance. COBIT provides a comprehensive set of guidelines for managing and controlling IT processes, ensuring that IT services support business goals and comply with regulatory requirements. It is particularly useful for organizations that are focused on managing IT risks, ensuring compliance, and aligning IT with business strategy.

In addition to ITIL, ISO/IEC 20000, and COBIT, organizations may also choose to adopt frameworks such as Lean IT, Agile, and DevOps to complement their ITSM practices. Lean IT is an approach that focuses on maximizing value and minimizing waste by streamlining IT processes. It draws heavily on the principles of Lean manufacturing, emphasizing efficiency, process optimization, and the elimination of non-value-added activities. Lean IT helps organizations reduce costs, improve service delivery, and increase customer satisfaction by focusing on continuous improvement and the efficient use of resources.

Agile IT, on the other hand, is a framework that prioritizes flexibility, collaboration, and iterative development. It is commonly used in software development environments, but its principles can be applied to IT service management as well. Agile emphasizes the importance of responding quickly to changing business needs, delivering value incrementally, and fostering strong collaboration between cross-functional teams. Agile ITSM enables organizations to be more adaptive, responsive, and customer-centric, ensuring that IT services are delivered in a way that meets the evolving needs of the business.

DevOps is another framework that has gained popularity in recent years, particularly in environments where rapid development and continuous delivery of software are essential. DevOps is a cultural and technical movement that bridges the gap between development and operations teams, encouraging collaboration, automation, and continuous integration. By breaking down silos between development and operations, DevOps helps organizations deliver IT services more quickly, with greater quality and reliability. In the context of ITSM, DevOps enables faster deployment of services, more efficient management of incidents and changes, and a stronger focus on customer feedback and continuous improvement.

The choice of ITSM framework depends on a variety of factors, including the size of the organization, the complexity of its IT environment, its business objectives, and its existing processes. Some organizations may choose to adopt a single framework, while others may integrate multiple frameworks to create a hybrid approach that best meets their needs. For example, an organization may choose to adopt ITIL for its overall service management practices, while also incorporating Agile principles to ensure flexibility and responsiveness in its development processes. Similarly, an organization focused on IT governance and risk management may choose to use COBIT alongside ITIL to ensure that its IT services are aligned with regulatory requirements and business objectives.

Regardless of the specific framework or combination of frameworks an organization chooses, the importance of ITSM frameworks cannot be overstated. These frameworks provide the structure, guidance, and best practices necessary for managing IT services in a way that delivers value to the business and its customers. By adopting a framework, organizations can standardize their processes, improve service quality, enhance customer satisfaction, and ensure that their IT services are aligned with business goals. Furthermore, frameworks like ITIL and ISO/IEC 20000 provide organizations with a means of measuring and benchmarking their ITSM processes, helping them identify areas for improvement and implement continuous improvement practices.

The integration of ITSM frameworks also plays a significant role in promoting a culture of collaboration within an organization. As IT service management requires coordination between various teams, such as IT operations, development, security, and customer support, frameworks like ITIL and DevOps emphasize the importance of collaboration and communication. By breaking down silos and fostering a collaborative culture, organizations can enhance the efficiency and effectiveness of their IT services, ensuring that they meet the needs of the business and deliver a positive customer experience.

In an increasingly digital world, the ability to deliver high-quality IT services is critical to the success of any organization. ITSM frameworks provide the roadmap for achieving this goal by offering structured approaches to service delivery, continuous improvement, and alignment with business objectives. Organizations that adopt and implement ITSM frameworks are better equipped to navigate the complexities of modern IT environments, improve service quality, and stay competitive in a rapidly changing business landscape. As technology continues to evolve, the role of ITSM frameworks in shaping the future of IT service management will only continue to grow in importance.

The ITIL Framework: Foundations and Structure

The ITIL (Information Technology Infrastructure Library) framework is one of the most widely adopted frameworks for IT Service Management (ITSM) worldwide. It provides organizations with a comprehensive set of best practices for delivering IT services in a way that aligns with business goals and meets customer needs. Originally developed by the British government in the 1980s, ITIL has evolved significantly over the years to address the growing complexities of modern IT environments. At its core, ITIL is designed to ensure that IT services are delivered efficiently, effectively, and with continuous improvement, while also fostering a customer-centric approach.

The foundation of ITIL is based on the principle that IT should not be seen merely as a technical support function but as a strategic asset that enables business success. By providing a set of guidelines, processes, and practices, ITIL ensures that IT services are managed in a way that delivers maximum value to the organization. ITIL emphasizes the importance of aligning IT services with the needs of the business and its customers. This approach helps organizations not only to manage their IT resources effectively but also to focus on providing value through their services. The framework fosters a holistic view of IT management, recognizing that every stage of a service's lifecycle, from strategy to design to continual improvement, plays a critical role in its success.

One of the key aspects of the ITIL framework is its focus on the service lifecycle. The service lifecycle is a model that outlines the different stages that an IT service goes through, from its initial conception to its eventual retirement. The lifecycle consists of five stages: Service Strategy, Service Design, Service Transition, Service Operation, and Continual Service Improvement. Each of these stages is integral to the overall management and delivery of IT services, ensuring that services are designed and delivered in a structured, efficient, and customer-focused manner. The service lifecycle helps organizations create a comprehensive approach to ITSM, enabling them to manage services effectively throughout their entire lifecycle and adapt to changing business needs over time.

The Service Strategy stage is the foundation of the service lifecycle. This stage focuses on understanding the business needs and ensuring that IT services are aligned with those needs. It involves defining the objectives and goals of IT services, as well as developing a strategy for delivering those services. The Service Strategy stage helps organizations assess the potential value of different services, prioritize them based on business requirements, and ensure that the service portfolio is optimized to meet both short-term and long-term business goals. By focusing on the strategic alignment of IT services, organizations can ensure that their IT investments contribute to the achievement of broader business objectives.

Following the Service Strategy stage is Service Design, which focuses on the planning and creation of new IT services or the improvement of existing services. During this phase, ITIL emphasizes the importance of designing services that meet business needs while also ensuring that they are scalable, secure, and cost-effective. The Service Design stage involves not only technical design but also designing processes, policies, and procedures to ensure that services are delivered efficiently and effectively. This stage helps organizations ensure that new services are thoroughly planned before implementation, minimizing the risk of failure and ensuring that services are capable of delivering the intended value to the business.

Once services have been designed, they move into the Service Transition phase. This phase is focused on implementing and deploying services into the live environment. Service Transition ensures that the transition from development to production is smooth, minimizing disruptions and ensuring that services are properly tested and validated before they go live. This stage also includes change management, release management, and configuration management, which are essential for ensuring that changes to IT services are managed in a controlled and predictable manner. The Service Transition stage helps organizations mitigate risks associated with service deployment, ensuring that services are stable, reliable, and ready to meet customer expectations once they are fully operational.

The next stage in the service lifecycle is Service Operation, which focuses on the day-to-day management of IT services. During this phase, IT services are delivered and supported to ensure that they are performing as expected and meeting business needs. Service Operation includes key ITIL processes such as incident management, problem management, request fulfillment, and access management. These processes are designed to ensure that services are provided with minimal disruption, that issues are resolved promptly, and that customers receive the support they need. Service Operation is critical for maintaining the stability and reliability of IT services, and its success directly impacts customer satisfaction and business performance.

Finally, Continual Service Improvement (CSI) is an ongoing process that runs throughout the service lifecycle. CSI focuses on identifying opportunities for improving the quality, efficiency, and effectiveness of IT services. This stage encourages organizations to continuously assess their services and processes, using data and feedback to drive improvements. CSI helps organizations adapt to changing business environments, address emerging challenges, and optimize service delivery. By incorporating continual improvement into every stage of the service lifecycle, organizations can ensure that their IT services evolve to meet the growing needs of the business and its customers.

The structure of ITIL is designed to be flexible, allowing organizations to tailor its practices to their specific needs and environments. The framework is not a one-size-fits-all solution but rather a set of best practices that can be adapted and integrated into an organization's existing processes. ITIL is also designed to be scalable, meaning it can be applied to organizations of all sizes, from small businesses to large enterprises. This flexibility makes ITIL a versatile framework for organizations looking to improve their IT service management practices and deliver greater value through their IT services.

In addition to its core lifecycle stages, ITIL also provides a set of guiding principles and processes that support effective service management. These include processes for managing incidents, problems, changes, configurations, and service levels, among others. Each of these processes is designed to ensure that IT services are delivered in a structured and controlled manner, minimizing risk and improving service quality. ITIL also emphasizes the importance of service measurement and performance management, helping organizations track and evaluate the effectiveness of their services and make data-driven decisions for improvement.

Since its inception, ITIL has undergone several updates, with each version reflecting the evolving needs of organizations and the changing landscape of IT. The latest version, ITIL 4, introduced a more flexible and adaptive approach to IT service management. ITIL 4 focuses on integrating service management with modern practices such as Agile, DevOps, and Lean. This updated approach recognizes the need for organizations to be more agile, collaborative, and customer-focused, aligning IT services with business value and fostering a culture of continuous improvement. ITIL 4 introduces new concepts such as the Service Value System (SVS) and the Service Value Chain, which help organizations understand how various components of service management contribute to overall business success.

The ITIL framework has proven to be a valuable tool for organizations seeking to optimize their IT service management practices. Its structured approach to service management, combined with its focus on continual improvement and customer satisfaction, has made it a popular choice for organizations of all sizes. By adopting ITIL, organizations can ensure that their IT services are managed in a way that maximizes value, minimizes risks, and aligns with business objectives. As the IT landscape continues to evolve, ITIL remains a key framework for organizations looking to stay competitive and deliver high-quality IT services that meet the demands of the modern business environment.

ITIL Service Strategy

Service Strategy is one of the five key stages in the ITIL service lifecycle, playing a crucial role in shaping how IT services are delivered, managed, and aligned with the business objectives. At its core, Service Strategy is about understanding business goals, defining the IT services that will enable these goals, and ensuring that these services provide value to both the organization and its customers. This stage helps establish the framework for delivering services that are not only effective but also aligned with the long-term vision and objectives of the business. Service Strategy enables organizations to make informed decisions about which services to provide, how to deliver them efficiently, and how to measure their success over time.

One of the primary objectives of Service Strategy is to ensure that IT services are directly aligned with the business needs. Organizations are constantly faced with changing market conditions, evolving technologies, and shifting customer demands. Service Strategy helps organizations respond to these challenges by providing a structured approach to identifying the services that will provide the most value. By focusing on understanding business needs, Service Strategy ensures that IT services are not just reactive but are proactively designed to support the broader goals of the organization. This alignment between IT and business objectives is crucial for delivering services that meet customer expectations, drive business success, and contribute to a competitive advantage in the marketplace.

In Service Strategy, the process begins with a comprehensive assessment of the organization's goals, competitive landscape, and market dynamics. This understanding forms the basis for identifying which services will be most valuable to the business. For instance, Service Strategy involves analyzing the current service portfolio, understanding customer needs, and determining where improvements or new services might be needed. It also requires a focus on managing risks and understanding how different services can support the overall business strategy. This strategic approach ensures that IT services are not developed in isolation but are integrated into the business's overarching plans.

A key concept in Service Strategy is the service portfolio, which is the complete set of IT services that an organization provides. The service portfolio includes services at different stages of their lifecycle: from new services that are being developed to services that are being retired. Service Strategy helps organizations manage their service portfolio by making informed decisions about which services to continue, improve, or discontinue. The service portfolio management process is essential for ensuring that resources are allocated effectively and that services remain relevant to the business's evolving needs. This process also involves prioritizing services based on their value to the business and ensuring that they are adequately funded and resourced.

Service Strategy also focuses on the financial management of IT services, ensuring that services are delivered in a cost-effective manner. Financial management in Service Strategy includes budgeting, accounting, and charging for IT services. It helps organizations understand the cost of providing services and determine how to price them appropriately. By managing the financial aspects of IT services, organizations can ensure that they are delivering value while maintaining financial sustainability. This is particularly important in ensuring that services are affordable, both for the organization and for its customers, while still meeting the required service levels and quality standards.

Another important aspect of Service Strategy is demand management. Demand management focuses on understanding and forecasting the demand for IT services, ensuring that the organization can scale its services to meet customer needs without overextending resources. It involves analyzing historical data, identifying patterns in service usage, and forecasting future demand to ensure that the organization is prepared for both expected and unexpected increases in demand. Demand management helps organizations balance service capacity with customer needs, ensuring that IT resources are utilized efficiently and that service levels are maintained even during periods of high demand.

Service Strategy also includes the development of a clear value proposition for IT services. The value proposition defines the benefits that each IT service will deliver to customers and the business. It helps stakeholders understand why a particular service is important and how it will support the achievement of business objectives. The value proposition is critical for building support for IT services within the organization and for ensuring that customers understand the value they will receive. It serves as the foundation for service marketing, enabling organizations to communicate the benefits of their services to both internal and external stakeholders.

A key element of Service Strategy is ensuring that IT services are capable of delivering value over time. This involves continuous assessment of the services in the portfolio to ensure they remain aligned with business needs and customer expectations. By regularly reviewing the service portfolio, organizations can identify opportunities for improvement and make adjustments to services as necessary. This ongoing evaluation ensures that services evolve in line with changing business requirements, technological advancements, and customer feedback.

Service Strategy also emphasizes the importance of governance and compliance in the management of IT services. Governance in this context refers to the processes, policies, and controls that ensure IT services are delivered in accordance with organizational objectives, regulatory requirements, and industry best practices. It involves establishing clear roles and responsibilities, defining decision-making processes, and ensuring that service delivery is in line with both internal and external standards. Compliance ensures that IT services meet relevant legal, regulatory, and contractual obligations, mitigating the risk of non-compliance and ensuring that services are delivered in a secure and ethical manner.

Another important aspect of Service Strategy is the focus on creating a culture of continuous improvement. While Service Strategy sets the foundation for service delivery, it also encourages a mindset of ongoing evaluation and refinement. The services in the portfolio are regularly reviewed to identify areas where enhancements can be made, either by improving efficiency, increasing quality, or adapting to changing market conditions. By fostering a culture of continuous improvement, Service Strategy helps organizations stay agile and responsive, ensuring that services continue to provide value as the business and its environment evolve.

The strategic nature of Service Strategy means that it requires strong leadership and collaboration across the organization. Executives, service managers, and other key stakeholders must work together to ensure that the services being developed and delivered align with the business's overall strategy. Effective communication, decision-making, and collaboration are essential for the success of Service Strategy, as it involves multiple departments and stakeholders working toward common goals.

In the context of ITIL, Service Strategy is not just a one-time exercise but an ongoing process that continues throughout the lifecycle of IT services. As business needs change, new opportunities arise, and new technologies are introduced, Service Strategy ensures that IT services remain flexible and adaptable, capable of evolving with the business and its customers. Through continuous assessment, alignment with business goals, and a focus on delivering value, Service Strategy helps organizations navigate the complexities of modern IT environments and deliver services that contribute to the success of the business.

ITIL Service Design

Service Design is a critical phase in the ITIL service lifecycle, focusing on the creation and planning of new IT services, as well as the improvement of existing services. It plays a pivotal role in ensuring that services are designed in a way that not only meets the business requirements but also delivers value to customers while being cost-effective, secure, and sustainable. Service Design ensures that the service is well thought out before it is implemented, mitigating the risks of failure and ensuring a smooth transition into production. By concentrating on the design and planning aspects of IT services, Service Design helps organizations create services that are aligned with their business goals, operational needs, and customer expectations.

One of the primary objectives of Service Design is to ensure that services meet the agreed-upon service levels and are capable of delivering the desired business outcomes. This involves considering both the technical and non-technical aspects of service delivery, such as scalability, reliability, security, and compliance. Service Design goes beyond simply creating the technical components of a service; it also addresses the organizational processes, roles, and responsibilities required to deliver the service efficiently and effectively. The goal is to ensure that every aspect of the service, from the underlying technology to the processes that support it, is designed to function cohesively and deliver maximum value to the business and its customers.

A key element of Service Design is the creation of a service design package, which serves as a comprehensive blueprint for the service.

This package includes all the necessary details about the service, such as its architecture, service levels, security requirements, and operational procedures. The service design package ensures that all stakeholders, including business managers, service owners, and technical teams, have a clear understanding of what the service will entail and how it will be delivered. This package is vital for ensuring that the service is implemented correctly, meets business needs, and aligns with customer expectations. The service design package also serves as a reference point for managing changes to the service throughout its lifecycle, ensuring that any modifications are properly documented and communicated.

In Service Design, the design of the service itself is only one component. The design of the service management processes is equally important. Service Design ensures that the processes needed to deliver and support the service are carefully planned and defined. This includes processes for incident management, problem management, change management, and service level management, among others. By designing these processes in tandem with the service itself, organizations can ensure that the service is not only technically sound but also supported by a robust set of processes that will allow it to operate smoothly and efficiently in the long term.

One of the most important aspects of Service Design is its focus on ensuring that the service is both scalable and flexible. In today's fast-paced business environment, organizations must be able to adapt quickly to changing demands and new technologies. Service Design ensures that services are designed with the capacity to scale as needed, whether in terms of users, transactions, or geographical reach. This scalability is essential for ensuring that the service can grow with the business and continue to deliver value as the organization evolves. Flexibility is equally important, as it allows the service to be adapted or modified in response to changing business requirements, customer needs, or technological advancements.

Security is another crucial consideration in Service Design. As organizations increasingly rely on technology to drive their operations, the risk of cyber threats and data breaches has become a significant concern. Service Design ensures that security is integrated into the service from the outset, rather than being an afterthought. This involves considering the security requirements of the service, such as access control, data protection, and encryption, and ensuring that these requirements are incorporated into the design. By addressing security at the design stage, organizations can mitigate the risk of security breaches and ensure that their services are compliant with relevant regulations and industry standards.

Service Design also emphasizes the importance of user experience (UX) and customer satisfaction. A well-designed service should not only meet the functional requirements of the business but also provide a positive experience for users and customers. Service Design takes into account the usability of the service, ensuring that it is intuitive, easy to navigate, and aligned with the needs of its users. This focus on the user experience helps organizations deliver services that are not only effective but also engaging and user-friendly, which ultimately leads to greater customer satisfaction and loyalty.

Another critical component of Service Design is the integration of IT services with other parts of the organization. IT services rarely exist in isolation, and they must often interact with other business functions, such as sales, marketing, finance, and customer support. Service Design ensures that services are designed with this integration in mind, allowing for seamless collaboration between IT and other departments. This collaboration is essential for ensuring that the service meets the broader needs of the business and that all stakeholders are aligned in their goals and expectations.

As part of its holistic approach, Service Design also addresses the environmental and sustainability aspects of service delivery. In today's increasingly eco-conscious world, organizations are under growing pressure to reduce their environmental impact and adopt sustainable practices. Service Design ensures that services are designed with sustainability in mind, whether that means optimizing energy usage, reducing waste, or adopting environmentally friendly technologies. By considering sustainability in the design phase, organizations can not only meet regulatory requirements but also enhance their reputation as responsible corporate citizens.

Service Design is also responsible for the development of a robust service catalog, which is a comprehensive list of all the IT services available to users. The service catalog provides transparency into the services offered by IT and serves as a communication tool between IT and the business. It helps users understand what services are available, how to access them, and what the expected service levels are. A well-constructed service catalog is an essential part of Service Design, as it helps ensure that users are aware of the services available to them and can access the support they need quickly and efficiently.

Effective communication is essential throughout the Service Design process. Service Design involves a wide range of stakeholders, including business leaders, service owners, technical teams, and customers. By fostering clear and continuous communication between all parties, Service Design ensures that the final service meets the expectations of both the business and the customers it serves. This collaborative approach helps identify potential issues early in the design phase and ensures that the service is aligned with the organization's overall strategy.

Service Design plays a crucial role in ensuring that IT services are not only technically sound but also aligned with business goals, customer needs, and industry standards. It addresses a wide range of factors, from scalability and security to user experience and sustainability. By providing a structured and comprehensive approach to service design, organizations can ensure that their services are effective, reliable, and able to meet the evolving needs of the business. Ultimately, Service Design is about creating services that not only support business objectives but also enhance customer satisfaction and contribute to the long-term success of the organization.

ITIL Service Transition

Service Transition is a critical phase in the ITIL service lifecycle that focuses on the planning, coordination, and management of changes to IT services as they are moved from development to production. This phase is responsible for ensuring that newly designed or modified services are implemented smoothly, efficiently, and without disruption to existing operations. It is a bridge between the design and operation stages of the service lifecycle, providing the necessary mechanisms for the seamless introduction of services, as well as the integration of new technology, processes, and capabilities into the live environment. The goal of Service Transition is to ensure that the delivery of new or changed services is both predictable and reliable, minimizing risks, downtime, and service interruptions.

One of the primary objectives of Service Transition is to ensure that services are transitioned into production without disrupting existing services or causing negative impacts to the organization. This requires careful planning and a clear understanding of both the technical and business requirements of the service being transitioned. Service Transition includes a range of activities, from detailed testing and validation to communication and training, all aimed at ensuring that the service will perform as expected once it is operational. These activities help organizations manage the complexity and risks associated with implementing new services or making changes to existing ones, ensuring that the transition process is as smooth and efficient as possible.

A key component of Service Transition is change management. Changes to IT services can range from small updates and patches to large-scale modifications and new service introductions. Regardless of the size or complexity, every change needs to be carefully planned, tested, and communicated to ensure that it does not disrupt existing services or negatively impact the business. Change management helps to ensure that all changes are handled in a structured and controlled manner, reducing the risk of unexpected issues arising during or after the transition. This process includes assessing the impact of changes, obtaining approval from relevant stakeholders, and ensuring that the changes are implemented according to plan. By having a formalized change management process in place, organizations can ensure that changes are made with minimal disruption to business operations.

Release management is another important aspect of Service Transition. Release management focuses on ensuring that new or updated services are released into the live environment in a controlled and efficient manner. This includes everything from packaging and distributing the service to ensuring that it is properly deployed and configured in the live environment. Release management ensures that new services or changes to existing services are delivered consistently, meeting quality standards and being properly integrated with existing IT systems and infrastructure. Release management also involves ensuring that proper documentation and support materials are in place to help IT teams manage the service once it is live, as well as ensuring that users are trained on how to use the new service effectively.

Testing and validation are integral parts of the Service Transition phase. Before a new or changed service is released into production, it must be thoroughly tested to ensure that it meets the specified requirements and performs as expected. This includes functional testing, performance testing, and security testing, among other activities. Testing ensures that the service is stable, reliable, and ready for deployment, and that it does not introduce any unforeseen issues that could disrupt business operations. In addition to functional testing, Service Transition also emphasizes the importance of validation, which ensures that the service meets the business needs it was designed to fulfill. Validation checks whether the service will deliver the expected value to customers and the organization, ensuring that it aligns with the original service strategy and design.

Knowledge management also plays a significant role in Service Transition. As new services are introduced or existing services are changed, it is essential to ensure that all relevant knowledge is documented and shared with the appropriate teams. This includes technical documentation, process guides, and lessons learned from previous transitions. Knowledge management ensures that IT teams have the information they need to manage and support the service effectively once it is live. By capturing and sharing this knowledge, organizations can reduce the time and effort required to manage services, as well as avoid repeating mistakes from previous transitions.

Service Transition also involves ensuring that all stakeholders are properly engaged and informed throughout the transition process. Effective communication is essential for ensuring that everyone involved in the transition, from technical teams to business stakeholders, understands what is happening, when it is happening, and what impact it may have. Communication ensures that all parties are aligned in their expectations, which helps to reduce misunderstandings and manage any resistance to change. Properly managing stakeholder expectations is crucial for a successful transition, as it helps to ensure that everyone is on board with the changes and that any concerns are addressed in a timely and effective manner.

The role of service management tools is also critical in the Service Transition phase. These tools support the planning, coordination, and execution of transition activities, enabling teams to manage tasks, track progress, and ensure that all aspects of the transition are carried out as planned. Service management tools provide visibility into the status of the transition, helping to identify any issues or risks early on and allowing teams to take corrective action before they become problems. These tools also help automate many aspects of the transition process, reducing the likelihood of human error and improving overall efficiency.

Service Transition also emphasizes the importance of post-transition reviews. After a service has been deployed into production, it is essential to assess the effectiveness of the transition and identify any areas for improvement. Post-transition reviews involve gathering feedback from stakeholders, analyzing performance data, and identifying lessons learned. This feedback loop helps organizations continually improve their transition processes, ensuring that future transitions are smoother, faster, and more effective. By incorporating lessons learned from previous transitions, organizations can refine their strategies and minimize the risks associated with future service deployments.

In a rapidly changing technological landscape, Service Transition becomes even more critical. The need to deliver new services quickly and efficiently, while maintaining operational stability, has never been greater. Organizations are under constant pressure to innovate and meet customer demands, and Service Transition provides the structure and discipline needed to manage this process effectively. By ensuring that new or changed services are delivered in a controlled and systematic manner, organizations can not only reduce the risk of failure but also ensure that their IT services continue to meet the evolving needs of the business and its customers.

Service Transition is a vital phase in the ITIL service lifecycle, helping organizations manage the complexities and risks associated with the introduction of new or modified services. Through careful planning, structured change management, thorough testing and validation, and effective communication, Service Transition ensures that services are implemented smoothly and that the organization can realize the expected benefits of its IT investments. By focusing on minimizing disruption, managing stakeholder expectations, and leveraging service management tools, organizations can ensure that their services are delivered efficiently and effectively, providing maximum value to the business and its customers.

ITIL Service Operation

Service Operation is one of the key stages in the ITIL service lifecycle, focusing on the day-to-day management of IT services to ensure that they are delivered effectively and efficiently to meet business requirements. This phase is centered on maintaining the stability and reliability of IT services, ensuring that they perform as expected, and resolving any issues that may arise during normal service operations. Service Operation plays a crucial role in the overall success of IT service management by ensuring that services are consistently available, reliable, and responsive to the needs of the business and its customers. It bridges the gap between the design and continual improvement phases, ensuring that services are consistently delivered according to the expectations set in previous stages of the service lifecycle.

At the heart of Service Operation is the delivery of IT services in a way that minimizes disruption and maximizes value for both the organization and its customers. Service Operation involves managing the operation of IT services to ensure that they function effectively and efficiently. This includes ensuring that service levels are met, addressing issues as they arise, and continuously monitoring the performance of services to identify potential problems before they escalate. By focusing on maintaining the health and stability of IT services, Service Operation helps organizations minimize the impact of service disruptions on business operations and ensures that services are delivered in a manner that meets customer expectations.

One of the most important components of Service Operation is incident management. Incidents are unplanned disruptions to IT services that cause service degradation or unavailability. Incident management ensures that incidents are handled promptly and efficiently, minimizing the impact on the business. The objective of incident management is to restore normal service operation as quickly as possible, thereby minimizing downtime and ensuring that the organization's IT services are available when needed. Incident management processes typically involve logging and categorizing incidents, prioritizing them based on their severity, and coordinating resources to resolve them. Effective incident management requires clear communication with end-users, fast response times, and the ability to resolve issues efficiently, ensuring that services are restored with minimal disruption.

Problem management is another critical process within Service Operation. While incident management focuses on addressing immediate disruptions, problem management is concerned with identifying and eliminating the root causes of recurring incidents. Problem management aims to prevent incidents from occurring in the first place by identifying underlying issues and implementing solutions to eliminate them. This proactive approach helps reduce the number of incidents over time and improves the overall stability of IT services. Problem management involves conducting root cause analysis, developing permanent fixes for recurring issues, and ensuring that solutions are properly implemented and tested to prevent future occurrences. By addressing the root causes of problems, organizations can achieve long-term improvements in service reliability and performance.

Change management is also an essential part of Service Operation. Change management ensures that changes to IT services and infrastructure are implemented in a controlled and predictable manner, minimizing the risk of disruption and service degradation. In a dynamic IT environment, changes are inevitable, but they must be carefully managed to avoid unintended consequences. Change management processes include assessing the potential impact of changes, obtaining approval from stakeholders, planning and scheduling the changes, and ensuring that they are implemented without causing unnecessary disruption. Effective change management ensures that changes are made in a way that minimizes risk while allowing the organization to continue to innovate and adapt to evolving business needs.

Another key aspect of Service Operation is the service desk, which serves as the primary point of contact between IT and its customers. The service desk is responsible for handling service requests, incidents, and inquiries from end-users. It acts as the central hub for IT support and plays a crucial role in ensuring that IT services are delivered effectively and efficiently. The service desk helps manage the communication between IT and users, ensuring that users are kept informed about the status of their requests and incidents. Additionally, the service desk is responsible for logging and categorizing service requests and incidents, ensuring that they are properly tracked and managed. A well-functioning service desk is essential for maintaining customer satisfaction and ensuring that IT services are delivered in a timely and responsive manner.

Monitoring and event management are critical functions within Service Operation. Monitoring ensures that IT services are continuously observed to detect any potential issues that may arise. This includes tracking service performance, availability, and capacity to identify any deviations from expected behavior. Event management focuses on detecting and managing events, which are notifications of changes in the state of a service or system. By monitoring services and events, organizations can proactively identify issues before they escalate into serious problems. Early detection of potential issues allows IT teams to take corrective action before service disruptions occur, helping to maintain the stability and reliability of IT services.

Service Operation also includes the management of access and security. Access management ensures that only authorized users are allowed to access specific services and resources, protecting the organization's IT infrastructure from unauthorized access or misuse. Security management focuses on ensuring that services are protected from potential threats, including cyberattacks, data breaches, and other security risks. Together, access management and security management help ensure that IT services are safe and secure, protecting both the organization's data and its customers' information.

In addition to managing incidents and problems, Service Operation also focuses on managing service levels and ensuring that agreed-upon service levels are met. Service level management ensures that IT services meet the performance expectations defined in service level agreements (SLAs) and that any deviations from these expectations are addressed promptly. By measuring and monitoring service performance, service level management helps organizations ensure that services are delivered at the required level of quality and availability. This process also involves reviewing and renegotiating SLAs as necessary to ensure that they remain aligned with changing business requirements and customer expectations.

One of the critical challenges faced by organizations during the Service Operation phase is balancing the need for innovation and improvement with the need for stability and reliability. While organizations are constantly striving to innovate and improve their IT services, they must also ensure that existing services continue to operate smoothly and without disruption. This requires effective coordination between different IT teams, including development, operations, and support, to ensure that changes and improvements are introduced in a controlled and predictable manner. By maintaining this balance, organizations can continue to deliver high-quality IT services while also evolving to meet the changing needs of the business.

Service Operation is an ongoing, dynamic phase that requires constant attention and management. IT services are often subject to fluctuations in demand, changes in technology, and shifts in business requirements. Therefore, Service Operation requires a flexible, adaptive approach to ensure that services remain responsive to these changes while maintaining stability and reliability. By focusing on incident and problem management, change control, service desk support, monitoring, and service level management, organizations can ensure that their IT services continue to meet the needs of the business and deliver value to customers.

The effectiveness of Service Operation directly impacts the overall success of IT service management. By ensuring that IT services are available, reliable, and responsive to customer needs, Service Operation plays a vital role in maintaining the performance and reputation of IT services. Organizations that invest in well-designed and well-managed Service Operation processes can achieve greater operational efficiency, improved customer satisfaction, and a more resilient IT environment that can adapt to the evolving needs of the business.

ITIL Continual Service Improvement

Continual Service Improvement (CSI) is an essential phase in the ITIL service lifecycle, focused on ensuring that IT services continually evolve to meet changing business needs and customer expectations. This phase emphasizes the importance of ongoing assessment and refinement of services, processes, and performance to achieve long-term success and deliver greater value. CSI is not a one-time effort but a continuous process embedded throughout the service lifecycle, from the initial design and implementation to the eventual retirement of services. It involves using data, feedback, and performance metrics to drive improvements and enhance the overall quality and effectiveness of IT services. CSI aims to help organizations optimize their service delivery, reduce costs, improve efficiency, and ultimately align IT services with business objectives.

The core philosophy behind CSI is that no service is ever perfect, and there is always room for improvement. Even the best-performing services can benefit from periodic evaluation and refinement. The goal of CSI is not only to make incremental improvements but also to ensure that IT services adapt to the changing needs of the business, advances in technology, and shifts in customer expectations. This ongoing process of review and enhancement helps organizations remain competitive, agile, and capable of meeting the demands of a dynamic business environment.

A key aspect of CSI is the use of data and performance metrics to drive decision-making. Through systematic measurement and monitoring, organizations can assess the effectiveness of their services and identify areas that require improvement. CSI relies on various data sources, including service performance data, customer feedback, incident reports, and service level management metrics. By analyzing this data, organizations can gain valuable insights into service performance, identify trends, and pinpoint specific issues that need attention. This data-driven approach allows organizations to make informed decisions, prioritize improvements, and track progress over time.

CSI is often associated with the concept of the Deming Cycle, also known as Plan-Do-Check-Act (PDCA), which provides a structured approach to continual improvement. The PDCA cycle is a four-step process that can be applied to any service or process improvement effort. The first step, Plan, involves identifying opportunities for improvement, setting objectives, and developing a strategy to achieve them. The second step, Do, focuses on implementing the plan and making the necessary changes to services or processes. The third step, Check, involves evaluating the results of the changes, measuring their impact, and determining whether the objectives have been met. Finally, the Act step involves taking corrective actions based on the evaluation, standardizing successful improvements, and preparing for the next iteration of the improvement cycle. This iterative process ensures that improvements are continuously made and that services are always evolving to meet the needs of the business.

One of the primary goals of CSI is to optimize the efficiency and effectiveness of IT services. By identifying areas of inefficiency, organizations can streamline processes, reduce waste, and improve service delivery. For example, CSI may uncover opportunities to automate manual tasks, improve service desk operations, or refine incident management processes. These improvements help to reduce operational costs, increase productivity, and deliver a better customer experience. Additionally, CSI can help organizations optimize their use of resources, ensuring that IT services are delivered with the appropriate levels of capacity, performance, and reliability to meet business demands.

Customer satisfaction is a central focus of CSI. To deliver services that meet or exceed customer expectations, organizations must continuously evaluate and adjust their service offerings. CSI involves gathering customer feedback, whether through surveys, focus groups, or direct interactions, and using this information to make improvements that directly address customer needs and concerns. By engaging with customers and understanding their experiences, organizations can ensure that their IT services provide the value and quality that customers expect. This customer-centric approach is critical in today's competitive business landscape, where organizations must differentiate themselves by delivering exceptional customer experiences.

Another important aspect of CSI is aligning IT services with the overall business strategy. As business goals evolve, IT services must be able to adapt to new requirements and support new initiatives. CSI helps organizations assess whether existing services are still aligned with business objectives and whether any changes are needed. For example, as a business undergoes digital transformation, CSI can help identify the services that need to be upgraded or replaced to support new technologies or processes. By maintaining alignment with business strategy, CSI ensures that IT services continue to provide value and contribute to the success of the organization.

Service Level Management (SLM) plays a crucial role in CSI by ensuring that service levels are consistently met and that any deviations are addressed. SLM involves setting clear expectations for service performance, defining service level agreements (SLAs), and measuring service delivery against these agreements. CSI uses SLM data to assess whether services are meeting the agreed-upon standards and whether any adjustments are needed to improve service quality. If service levels are not being met, CSI can help identify the root causes and implement corrective actions, such as improving process efficiency or allocating additional resources to critical services. By continuously monitoring and improving service levels, CSI helps organizations maintain high-quality service delivery and improve customer satisfaction.

In addition to improving existing services, CSI is also involved in the retirement of services that are no longer needed or relevant. Over time, services may become obsolete due to changes in technology, business needs, or customer preferences. CSI ensures that the retirement process is managed effectively, minimizing the impact on customers and business operations. The decision to retire a service should be based on a thorough evaluation of its performance, its relevance to the business, and its ability to meet customer needs. CSI helps organizations make informed decisions about service retirement, ensuring that resources are allocated efficiently and that the transition to new services is smooth.

CSI also plays an important role in risk management. By continuously monitoring and assessing the performance of IT services, organizations can identify potential risks before they become significant issues. For example, CSI can uncover weaknesses in security, performance bottlenecks, or compliance gaps that need to be addressed. By proactively managing risks and implementing improvements, organizations can avoid service disruptions, data breaches, and other costly incidents. This proactive approach to risk management is essential in maintaining the stability and security of IT services, ensuring that the organization can meet its operational and strategic objectives without compromising on quality or security.

The implementation of CSI requires strong leadership and a culture of continuous improvement. Organizations need to foster an environment where improvement is seen as a constant and ongoing process, with every employee and team member playing a role in identifying opportunities for enhancement. Leadership must support and encourage improvement efforts, provide resources, and ensure that improvement initiatives are aligned with business goals. A culture of continuous improvement empowers employees to take ownership of service quality and to contribute to the success of the organization by driving positive change.

Continual Service Improvement is a fundamental aspect of ITIL that ensures IT services remain effective, relevant, and aligned with business needs over time. Through data-driven decision-making, customer feedback, and the application of structured improvement methodologies such as the PDCA cycle, CSI enables organizations to optimize their services, reduce costs, and enhance customer satisfaction. By fostering a culture of continuous improvement, organizations can ensure that their IT services continue to provide value, support business growth, and adapt to the evolving needs of the market.

Benefits of ITIL Adoption

Adopting ITIL (Information Technology Infrastructure Library) offers a wide range of benefits to organizations, whether they are large enterprises or small businesses. ITIL is a comprehensive framework for IT service management (ITSM) that provides a structured approach to delivering and managing IT services. The benefits of implementing ITIL extend far beyond mere process standardization. It enhances the alignment of IT services with business goals, improves service delivery, increases operational efficiency, and strengthens customer satisfaction, making it a valuable asset to any organization seeking to optimize its IT operations.

One of the primary benefits of ITIL adoption is the improvement in the alignment between IT services and business needs. Often, IT departments operate in isolation, focusing on technical requirements and infrastructure without fully understanding the strategic goals of the business. ITIL changes this dynamic by ensuring that IT services are closely aligned with business objectives. Through the service lifecycle framework, ITIL helps organizations define clear service strategies that meet customer demands and business requirements. It encourages IT professionals to work in close collaboration with business leaders, ensuring that technology is not only supporting the business but is an integral part of achieving its goals. This alignment leads to more effective decision-making, ensuring that IT investments drive business growth and help the organization remain competitive.

Another significant advantage of ITIL adoption is the enhancement of service delivery. By standardizing IT processes and introducing well-defined practices, ITIL ensures that services are delivered consistently and reliably. Service quality improves as ITIL guides organizations in the creation of service level agreements (SLAs) that set clear expectations for service performance and availability. These SLAs provide both IT teams and customers with an understanding of the level of service to expect, ensuring transparency and accountability. When services are consistently delivered according to agreed-upon standards, customers experience greater satisfaction, and the IT department builds a stronger reputation within the organization. ITIL's emphasis on continual service improvement further supports service delivery by encouraging regular assessments of services and their performance, ensuring they are optimized over time.

Efficiency is another area where ITIL adoption proves highly beneficial. By implementing best practices for IT service management, organizations can streamline their processes and eliminate inefficiencies. ITIL provides a clear structure for managing incidents, problems, changes, and configurations, helping IT teams respond more quickly to issues and minimize service disruptions. By standardizing workflows and automating repetitive tasks, organizations can reduce the time and resources spent on routine activities, allowing IT staff to focus on higher-value tasks. Additionally, ITIL promotes the idea of proactive problem management, where root causes of recurring issues are identified and addressed, further reducing the likelihood of disruptions. The result is an increase in the overall efficiency of IT operations, leading to cost savings and improved productivity.

The process-driven nature of ITIL adoption also enhances risk management. In any IT environment, there are inherent risks associated with service delivery, system failures, security breaches, and compliance issues. ITIL introduces a structured approach to risk management by ensuring that all processes are well-documented, monitored, and controlled. Change management processes, for example, help mitigate the risks associated with introducing changes to IT systems by ensuring that changes are thoroughly tested, approved, and implemented in a controlled manner. Similarly, incident management processes ensure that issues are addressed quickly, reducing the impact on business operations and preventing further disruptions. With ITIL, organizations are better equipped to identify potential risks early, implement preventive measures, and respond swiftly to any incidents, minimizing the overall impact on the business.

ITIL adoption also fosters a culture of continuous improvement. One of the key principles of ITIL is the concept of continual service improvement (CSI), which encourages organizations to regularly evaluate their services, processes, and performance to identify areas for enhancement. This philosophy drives organizations to constantly strive for higher service quality, better customer satisfaction, and more efficient operations. By utilizing feedback from customers, analyzing performance data, and conducting regular assessments, ITIL enables organizations to adapt to changing business needs and technological advancements. This focus on continuous improvement helps organizations stay agile and competitive, ensuring that IT services evolve in line with both internal and external changes.

Additionally, ITIL enhances the visibility of IT services within the organization. When IT services are managed using standardized processes and procedures, it becomes easier for both IT staff and business leaders to understand the status of services, their performance, and any issues that may arise. ITIL emphasizes the importance of documenting service delivery processes, creating clear service catalogs, and establishing performance metrics. This transparency allows for better decision-making, as managers can access detailed reports and performance indicators that highlight areas for improvement. Furthermore, ITIL promotes collaboration between IT and business units, creating a shared understanding of service performance and objectives, which ultimately fosters stronger relationships and better alignment between IT and the broader organization.

One of the critical benefits of ITIL adoption is the improvement in customer satisfaction. By focusing on service quality, reliability, and responsiveness, ITIL helps organizations deliver IT services that meet or exceed customer expectations. ITIL introduces practices such as service level management, which helps define clear expectations for service performance and availability, ensuring that customers receive the level of service they are promised. Furthermore, by emphasizing proactive problem management and efficient incident resolution, ITIL ensures that issues are addressed quickly, minimizing downtime and the negative impact on customers. Ultimately, the goal of ITIL is to enhance the customer experience, and organizations that adopt ITIL see improved relationships with customers, higher levels of trust, and increased customer loyalty.

In addition to improving service delivery and customer satisfaction, ITIL adoption helps organizations better manage their IT resources. ITIL provides a framework for managing both the technology and the human resources that support IT services. By following ITIL's best practices, organizations can optimize resource allocation, ensuring that IT assets are used efficiently and effectively. For example, ITIL's capacity management processes help organizations predict and manage demand, ensuring that the right resources are available when needed. ITIL's configuration management practices help organizations track and manage their IT assets, reducing the risk of unnecessary duplication or waste. This overall improvement in resource management leads to cost savings and a more effective IT operation.

Finally, ITIL adoption supports regulatory compliance and security management. In today's business environment, organizations face increasing pressure to comply with various regulations and ensure the security of their IT systems. ITIL helps organizations maintain compliance by providing well-defined processes and practices for managing security, data protection, and risk mitigation. For instance, change management and access management processes ensure that changes are made securely and that only authorized users have access to sensitive systems. By adhering to ITIL's best practices, organizations can ensure they meet the necessary legal and regulatory requirements while maintaining a secure IT environment.

The benefits of ITIL adoption are wide-ranging, impacting nearly every aspect of IT service management. By improving alignment with business objectives, enhancing service delivery, increasing efficiency, and fostering a culture of continuous improvement, ITIL helps organizations optimize their IT operations and provide greater value to both the business and its customers. Whether through better risk management, improved resource utilization, or enhanced customer satisfaction, ITIL enables organizations to achieve operational excellence and maintain a competitive edge in a rapidly evolving business environment.

The ISO/IEC 20000 Standard

The ISO/IEC 20000 standard is an internationally recognized framework for IT Service Management (ITSM) that provides organizations with a set of guidelines to establish, implement, operate, monitor, review, maintain, and improve their IT service management systems. This standard is designed to help organizations deliver high-quality IT services that meet customer needs, comply with regulatory requirements, and align with business objectives. Unlike other frameworks like ITIL, which focuses on best practices, ISO/IEC 20000 is a certifiable standard, meaning organizations can be audited and formally certified to demonstrate their compliance with its requirements. The ISO/IEC 20000 standard plays a crucial role in ensuring that IT services are delivered consistently, efficiently, and effectively, with a focus on continual improvement.

One of the key aspects of the ISO/IEC 20000 standard is its emphasis on integrating IT service management with the overall business strategy of an organization. In today's competitive and fast-paced business environment, it is not enough for IT departments to simply deliver services that work. They must align their operations with business goals to ensure that IT services contribute directly to business success. The ISO/IEC 20000 standard helps organizations achieve this alignment by providing a comprehensive framework for managing IT services. This includes defining service requirements, establishing clear roles and responsibilities, and ensuring that IT services support business objectives. The standard requires organizations to define their service management policy, objectives, and processes in a way that ensures IT services meet the needs of both the business and its customers.

The structure of the ISO/IEC 20000 standard is based on a lifecycle approach, similar to the ITIL framework, and is divided into several key sections that cover different aspects of IT service management. The standard provides a comprehensive set of requirements for establishing an effective service management system. It focuses on processes such as service design, service transition, service operation, and continual service improvement, ensuring that IT services are delivered in a controlled and systematic manner. By following this structured approach, organizations can ensure that their IT services are not only reliable but also capable of adapting to changing business needs over time.

One of the most important components of ISO/IEC 20000 is its focus on service quality. The standard requires organizations to define and measure key performance indicators (KPIs) to assess the effectiveness of their service management system. These KPIs include metrics related to service availability, incident resolution times, customer satisfaction, and other critical factors that directly impact the quality of IT services. By establishing these performance indicators, organizations can track their progress and identify areas where improvements are needed. This data-driven approach enables organizations to make informed decisions about their IT service management practices and prioritize efforts to enhance service quality.

Another significant aspect of the ISO/IEC 20000 standard is its focus on risk management. The standard requires organizations to identify, assess, and manage risks associated with IT service delivery. This includes risks related to security, compliance, performance, and other factors that can impact the reliability and effectiveness of IT services. By adopting a proactive approach to risk management, organizations can reduce the likelihood of service disruptions, security breaches, and other issues that could negatively affect their customers and business operations. The ISO/IEC 20000 standard provides a clear framework for managing these risks, helping organizations implement appropriate controls and preventive measures to minimize their exposure.

The standard also emphasizes the importance of continual service improvement (CSI). Continual improvement is a key principle of ISO/IEC 20000, as it ensures that IT services are regularly assessed and refined to meet evolving business needs and customer expectations. This approach is aligned with the concept of the Deming Cycle (Plan-Do-Check-Act), which encourages organizations to continuously evaluate their services and processes, implement changes, and measure the results. The ISO/IEC 20000 standard requires organizations to establish a process for reviewing their service management system, gathering feedback from customers and stakeholders, and identifying opportunities for improvement. This focus on continuous improvement helps organizations stay agile and responsive to changes in the business environment, ensuring that IT services continue to deliver value over time.

In addition to its focus on service quality, risk management, and continual improvement, ISO/IEC 20000 also provides requirements for the governance and management of IT services. The standard defines the roles and responsibilities of various stakeholders within the organization, ensuring that there is clear accountability for service management activities. It requires organizations to establish processes for managing incidents, changes, problems, and configurations, ensuring that these activities are carried out in a controlled and efficient manner. The standard also requires organizations to define their service portfolio, which includes a comprehensive catalog of the services they offer, along with the associated service levels, costs, and other relevant details. By providing a clear framework for service management governance, ISO/IEC 20000 helps organizations maintain control over their IT services and ensure that they are delivered according to agreed-upon standards.

One of the key benefits of adopting ISO/IEC 20000 is that it helps organizations improve customer satisfaction. By establishing clear processes, measuring performance, and ensuring that IT services are aligned with customer needs, organizations can deliver services that consistently meet or exceed customer expectations. The standard requires organizations to establish service level agreements (SLAs) that define the performance expectations for IT services, ensuring that customers know what to expect in terms of service availability, response times, and other critical factors. This transparency helps build trust between the IT department and its customers, leading to stronger relationships and higher levels of customer satisfaction.

Furthermore, ISO/IEC 20000 certification provides organizations with a competitive advantage. Achieving certification demonstrates to customers, partners, and stakeholders that the organization is committed to delivering high-quality IT services and following internationally recognized best practices. This certification can help organizations differentiate themselves from competitors, attract new customers, and build credibility in the marketplace. It also serves as evidence of the organization's commitment to continuous improvement, as the certification process requires ongoing assessment and refinement of service management practices.

The implementation of ISO/IEC 20000 can also lead to operational efficiencies. By standardizing service management processes, organizations can reduce duplication of effort, improve resource allocation, and streamline operations. This leads to cost savings, as well as the ability to respond more quickly to changes in customer needs or business requirements. The standard's focus on risk management also helps organizations reduce the costs associated with service disruptions, security incidents, and compliance violations, further contributing to operational efficiency.

ISO/IEC 20000 is a powerful tool for organizations seeking to improve their IT service management practices. By providing a structured, comprehensive framework for managing IT services, the standard ensures that services are aligned with business goals, delivered consistently and reliably, and continuously improved over time. Organizations that adopt ISO/IEC 20000 can enhance service quality, reduce risks, improve customer satisfaction, and achieve greater operational efficiency. Moreover, the certification process provides organizations with a clear benchmark for their service management practices, helping them maintain high standards and demonstrate their commitment to excellence. As businesses increasingly rely on technology to drive success, ISO/IEC 20000 provides the tools and framework needed to ensure that IT services continue to meet evolving business needs and deliver long-term value.

Aligning ITSM with ISO/IEC 20000

Aligning IT Service Management (ITSM) with the ISO/IEC 20000 standard is a strategic approach for organizations aiming to enhance the quality and efficiency of their IT services. ISO/IEC 20000 is an internationally recognized framework that provides a structured set of requirements for establishing, implementing, maintaining, and improving IT service management systems. When an organization adopts ITSM practices and aligns them with ISO/IEC 20000, it ensures that its IT services are not only aligned with business goals but are also delivered in a consistent, reliable, and cost-effective manner. This alignment helps organizations improve customer satisfaction, optimize service delivery, and achieve compliance with international standards, ultimately contributing to business success.

The first step in aligning ITSM with ISO/IEC 20000 is understanding the underlying principles and processes of both frameworks. ITSM is a broad concept that focuses on delivering and managing IT services in a way that meets the needs of the business and its customers. It includes various processes such as incident management, change management, service level management, and problem management. ISO/IEC 20000, on the other hand, is a certification standard for IT service management that provides a clear set of guidelines and requirements for achieving excellence in service delivery. While ITSM frameworks like ITIL offer best practices for managing IT services, ISO/IEC 20000 offers a formal, certifiable approach that ensures organizations meet globally recognized standards.

To align ITSM with ISO/IEC 20000, organizations must begin by assessing their current ITSM processes and identifying gaps in compliance with the ISO/IEC 20000 standard. ISO/IEC 20000 requires that organizations have a defined service management system (SMS) in place, covering all aspects of service delivery, from service design and operation to continual improvement. ITSM processes need to be evaluated and refined to meet these requirements. For example, organizations must ensure that service management policies are clearly defined, that roles and responsibilities are well-structured, and that resources are appropriately allocated to support service management activities. The goal is to ensure that the organization's service management system is comprehensive, effective, and aligned with the requirements of the ISO/IEC 20000 standard.

A significant area of focus in aligning ITSM with ISO/IEC 20000 is the integration of service management processes. ISO/IEC 20000 emphasizes the need for a holistic approach to service management, where all processes are interconnected and work together to deliver value to the business and its customers. For example, service level management, which is a critical ITSM process, must be integrated with other processes such as incident management, problem management, and change management. This ensures that service levels are consistently met, incidents are resolved efficiently, and changes are implemented without causing disruption. By aligning these processes with ISO/IEC 20000, organizations can ensure that they are managing IT services in a coordinated and effective manner.

Another important aspect of alignment is the documentation of processes and procedures. ISO/IEC 20000 requires that organizations document their service management practices to ensure that they are consistent, measurable, and repeatable. This documentation includes service management policies, procedures, and work instructions, which should be aligned with ITSM practices. By documenting these processes, organizations can ensure that their IT services are delivered in a controlled and systematic manner. Additionally, documentation is essential for meeting the audit and certification requirements of ISO/IEC 20000. Properly documented processes also facilitate continuous improvement, as they provide a basis for evaluating performance and identifying areas for enhancement.

A key component of ISO/IEC 20000 is continual service improvement (CSI). This principle is central to both ITSM and ISO/IEC 20000, as it emphasizes the need for organizations to continuously assess their services and processes to ensure that they remain effective and aligned with business goals. To align ITSM with ISO/IEC 20000, organizations must establish a structured approach to continual improvement, which includes regularly reviewing performance, identifying areas for improvement, and implementing changes to optimize service delivery. This approach ensures that services evolve in line with changing business needs, customer expectations, and technological advancements. By embedding continual improvement into their ITSM practices, organizations can ensure that their service management systems remain relevant and capable of delivering ongoing value.

Risk management is another area where aligning ITSM with ISO/IEC 20000 is crucial. The ISO/IEC 20000 standard requires organizations to identify and manage risks associated with service delivery, ensuring that services are delivered with a focus on security, compliance, and business continuity. ITSM processes such as change management and incident management play a critical role in managing risks by ensuring that changes are carefully planned and implemented, and that incidents are resolved quickly to minimize their impact on business operations. By aligning these ITSM processes with ISO/IEC 20000, organizations can ensure that they have a robust risk management framework in place to protect their IT services from potential threats.

Compliance and security are also vital aspects of aligning ITSM with ISO/IEC 20000. The standard requires organizations to demonstrate that they have implemented appropriate security controls to protect IT services and customer data. ITSM processes such as access management, incident management, and security management need to be aligned with ISO/IEC 20000 to ensure that services are secure, compliant, and protected against unauthorized access or data breaches. By aligning security practices with ISO/IEC 20000, organizations can enhance the overall security posture of their IT services, mitigate risks, and ensure that they comply with industry regulations and standards.

Aligning ITSM with ISO/IEC 20000 also has significant benefits for customer satisfaction. ISO/IEC 20000 requires organizations to establish clear service level agreements (SLAs) that define the performance expectations for IT services. By aligning ITSM processes with ISO/IEC 20000, organizations can ensure that they meet or exceed these service level expectations, resulting in improved service quality and customer satisfaction. Additionally, by adopting best practices for incident management, problem management, and change management, organizations can ensure that they resolve issues quickly and minimize disruptions to business operations. This leads to higher customer trust and loyalty, as well as a stronger reputation for delivering high-quality IT services.

The process of aligning ITSM with ISO/IEC 20000 also helps organizations improve operational efficiency. By standardizing and streamlining service management processes, organizations can reduce redundancy, improve resource allocation, and ensure that services are delivered in a cost-effective manner. The integration of ITSM practices with the ISO/IEC 20000 standard ensures that resources are used optimally, reducing waste and improving service delivery efficiency. This not only contributes to cost savings but also allows organizations to respond more quickly to changes in customer needs or market conditions.

In summary, aligning ITSM with ISO/IEC 20000 is a strategic approach that helps organizations optimize their IT services, improve service delivery, reduce risks, and enhance customer satisfaction. By integrating ITSM processes with the ISO/IEC 20000 framework, organizations can ensure that their IT services are managed effectively and consistently, while also complying with international standards. This alignment provides a solid foundation for continual improvement, allowing organizations to adapt to evolving business needs and remain competitive in an increasingly complex and dynamic IT landscape.

The Relationship Between ITIL and ISO/IEC 20000

The relationship between ITIL (Information Technology Infrastructure Library) and ISO/IEC 20000 is one of complementarity, where both frameworks serve as tools to guide organizations in managing and improving their IT services, but they do so in different ways. ITIL is a widely adopted best practice framework that focuses on providing a set of detailed processes and guidelines for managing IT services. In contrast, ISO/IEC 20000 is an international standard that provides formal requirements for an organization's IT service management system, aiming for a certifiable level of service quality and compliance with recognized international standards. While ITIL provides a flexible, practical approach to managing services, ISO/IEC 20000 offers a certification mechanism that helps organizations demonstrate their adherence to service management best practices, including those defined by ITIL.

One of the key distinctions between ITIL and ISO/IEC 20000 is their nature. ITIL is a collection of best practices that organizations can adopt to improve their service management processes. It is based on practical experience and focuses on improving the delivery and management of IT services, emphasizing process optimization, quality improvement, and customer satisfaction. ITIL is highly adaptable, allowing organizations to tailor its practices to their unique needs, resources, and goals. It offers a framework for continuous improvement by providing a structured approach to managing service design, transition, operation, and continual improvement.

ISO/IEC 20000, on the other hand, is an internationally recognized standard that sets out the requirements for an effective IT service management system. It is a formal certification standard, meaning that organizations can be audited and certified to demonstrate their compliance with the standard. The ISO/IEC 20000 standard is more prescriptive than ITIL, as it specifies the minimum criteria an organization must meet to achieve certification. These requirements cover a range of areas, including the establishment of a service management system, the definition of roles and responsibilities, the implementation of service level agreements, and the monitoring and measuring of service performance. The goal of ISO/IEC 20000 is to ensure that IT services are managed effectively, consistently, and in alignment with business objectives, while also meeting international service management best practices.

The relationship between ITIL and ISO/IEC 20000 becomes clear when we consider how organizations can use both frameworks together to improve their IT service management practices. While ITIL provides the guidance and best practices for managing services, ISO/IEC 20000 provides a formal structure and a set of requirements that ensure organizations are following a systematic, controlled approach to IT service management. Organizations can adopt ITIL's best practices and processes as part of their service management system and then use ISO/IEC 20000 as a benchmark to ensure that their practices meet the required standards for quality, performance, and continuous improvement. In essence, ITIL provides the "how" of service management, while ISO/IEC 20000 provides the "what" in terms of certification requirements.

Implementing ITIL practices and aligning them with ISO/IEC 20000 can help organizations achieve several important benefits. One of the most significant advantages is the ability to demonstrate to customers, partners, and stakeholders that the organization's IT service management processes are robust, compliant with international standards, and continuously improving. ISO/IEC 20000 certification serves as tangible evidence of the organization's commitment to high-quality service management, which can strengthen its reputation, attract new customers, and differentiate it from competitors. This certification is especially valuable in industries where regulatory compliance, security, and performance are critical, as it provides assurance that the organization is meeting industry standards and best practices.

In addition to improving credibility and customer trust, the relationship between ITIL and ISO/IEC 20000 helps organizations optimize their service management processes. By adopting ITIL's flexible best practices and aligning them with the requirements of ISO/IEC 20000, organizations can standardize their processes, streamline operations, and improve efficiency. For instance, by implementing ITIL's incident management and problem management processes in alignment with ISO/IEC 20000, organizations can ensure that they are efficiently resolving issues, minimizing service disruptions, and continuously improving their response to incidents. Similarly, by integrating ITIL's service level management practices with ISO/IEC 20000's requirements for service performance measurement and reporting, organizations can ensure that they are consistently meeting customer expectations and improving service quality over time.

Moreover, the combination of ITIL and ISO/IEC 20000 supports a culture of continual improvement. ITIL encourages organizations to assess their services and processes regularly, identifying areas for enhancement and implementing changes to optimize service delivery. ISO/IEC 20000, with its emphasis on monitoring and measuring service performance, provides the necessary structure to ensure that improvements are tracked, analyzed, and sustained over time. By aligning ITIL's focus on service improvement with ISO/IEC 20000's formal requirements for continual service improvement, organizations can create a feedback loop that drives ongoing enhancements in their service management processes.

ISO/IEC 20000 also helps organizations meet the challenges associated with maintaining consistency and compliance across different departments, teams, and locations. Because it provides a clear set of requirements and criteria for managing services, ISO/IEC 20000 ensures that organizations have a unified approach to IT service management, regardless of geographical location or team structure. ITIL, with its emphasis on process integration and collaboration between different IT functions, complements this approach by helping organizations foster cross-functional teamwork and break down silos within the organization. Together, ITIL and ISO/IEC 20000 help organizations deliver IT services that are not only effective and efficient but also standardized and compliant with industry best practices.

Another key area where ITIL and ISO/IEC 20000 complement each other is in risk management. Both frameworks emphasize the importance of identifying and mitigating risks associated with IT services, whether they are related to service disruptions, security breaches, or non-compliance with regulations. By implementing ITIL's best practices for change management, incident management, and problem management, organizations can reduce the likelihood of service failures and ensure that they are prepared to respond quickly to any issues that arise. At the same time, ISO/IEC 20000 provides a formal framework for identifying, assessing, and managing risks, ensuring that organizations have the necessary controls and measures in place to prevent and address potential risks to service delivery. By aligning both frameworks, organizations can strengthen their risk management practices and improve the overall resilience of their IT services.

The relationship between ITIL and ISO/IEC 20000 also extends to customer satisfaction and service delivery. ITIL provides organizations with a structured approach to managing service delivery, from defining service requirements to monitoring performance and resolving issues. ISO/IEC 20000, with its focus on service level management and performance measurement, ensures that organizations are meeting their customers' expectations and continuously improving their services. By adopting both frameworks, organizations can enhance their ability to deliver high-quality, reliable IT services that meet or exceed customer needs, leading to improved customer satisfaction and loyalty.

In summary, the relationship between ITIL and ISO/IEC 20000 is one of synergy, where ITIL provides the best practices and flexible approach for managing IT services, while ISO/IEC 20000 offers a formal framework for ensuring that these services meet international standards for quality and performance. Organizations that align ITIL with ISO/IEC 20000 can optimize their IT service management practices, improve service delivery, achieve certification, and enhance customer satisfaction. Together, these frameworks help organizations manage their IT services more effectively, reduce risks, and ensure continual improvement, all of which contribute to long-term success.

The COBIT Framework for IT Governance and Management

The COBIT (Control Objectives for Information and Related Technologies) framework is a comprehensive IT governance and management framework designed to provide organizations with a structured approach to managing and governing their information technology systems and processes. Developed by ISACA (Information Systems Audit and Control Association), COBIT is widely recognized as one of the leading frameworks for IT governance, risk management, and compliance. Its primary purpose is to help organizations ensure that IT aligns with their business objectives, delivers value, mitigates risks, and operates effectively and efficiently. COBIT provides a set of tools, guidelines, and best practices that enable organizations to optimize their IT resources and ensure that their IT systems and processes meet the necessary standards for governance, control, and performance.

COBIT's framework is built around a set of principles that focus on the integration of IT governance and management into the overall governance structure of the organization. The framework emphasizes the need for organizations to manage IT not just from a technical standpoint but as a strategic asset that plays a critical role in achieving business goals. It enables organizations to ensure that their IT systems and processes are aligned with business objectives, capable of delivering value to the business, and adequately managing risks associated with information technology. COBIT's approach to IT governance is holistic, addressing not only the technical aspects of IT but also the organizational, operational, and strategic dimensions of IT management.

At the core of the COBIT framework is its focus on the governance of information technology. COBIT helps organizations establish clear governance structures that define roles, responsibilities, and accountabilities for managing IT systems and processes. This includes ensuring that there is clear oversight of IT operations, strategic decision-making, and performance monitoring. By defining governance structures, COBIT helps organizations ensure that IT resources are effectively allocated, that IT projects are well-managed, and that IT performance is consistently monitored and evaluated. This ensures that IT investments are aligned with business priorities, and that IT delivers the expected value while minimizing risks and ensuring compliance with relevant regulations.

One of the key aspects of COBIT is its focus on risk management. The framework provides a structured approach for identifying, assessing, and managing risks related to IT operations and information security. In today's rapidly changing business environment, organizations face a wide range of risks associated with their IT systems, from cyber threats and data breaches to system failures and compliance violations. COBIT helps organizations develop a risk management strategy that enables them to identify potential threats, assess their impact, and implement controls and mitigation measures to reduce or eliminate those risks. This proactive approach to risk management ensures that organizations are better equipped to handle the challenges posed by information technology and maintain the security and integrity of their IT systems.

COBIT also places a strong emphasis on the importance of performance management. The framework provides guidelines for measuring and evaluating the performance of IT systems, processes, and resources to ensure that they are operating effectively and delivering value to the business. COBIT defines a set of performance metrics that organizations can use to assess the efficiency, effectiveness, and quality of their IT operations. These metrics include factors such as service availability, incident resolution times, and user satisfaction. By measuring performance against established benchmarks, organizations can identify areas for improvement, optimize their IT processes, and ensure that IT continues to contribute to business success.

The framework also emphasizes the need for compliance with laws, regulations, and industry standards. As organizations increasingly rely on IT to drive business operations, they must also comply with various legal and regulatory requirements related to data protection, information security, and financial reporting. COBIT helps organizations establish processes and controls that ensure compliance with these requirements, reducing the risk of non-compliance and the potential consequences of legal or regulatory violations. The framework provides guidelines for managing compliance across various areas of IT, including data privacy, information security, and financial governance, helping organizations mitigate the risks associated with non-compliance and avoid penalties or reputational damage.

Another key benefit of COBIT is its ability to promote transparency and accountability within the organization. By providing clear guidelines for IT governance and management, COBIT ensures that there is visibility into IT operations, decision-making processes, and performance. This transparency enables organizations to better manage their IT resources, track the progress of IT projects, and ensure that IT activities are aligned with business goals. It also helps to foster a culture of accountability, where IT leaders and teams are held responsible for delivering results, managing risks, and ensuring compliance. This accountability ensures that IT resources are used efficiently and effectively, and that IT projects deliver value to the business.

COBIT is also highly adaptable, allowing organizations to tailor its principles and processes to their specific needs and objectives. The framework provides a flexible approach to IT governance, enabling organizations to apply its guidelines in a way that is consistent with their unique business environment, industry requirements, and regulatory obligations. This flexibility ensures that COBIT can be applied across a wide range of industries and organizations, from large enterprises with complex IT environments to small businesses with more limited IT resources. Organizations can adopt the COBIT framework incrementally, starting with a few key processes and expanding it over time as their IT governance needs evolve.

Furthermore, COBIT facilitates the integration of IT governance and management with broader enterprise governance practices. The framework encourages organizations to integrate IT governance into their overall governance structures, ensuring that IT is managed as a key enabler of business success. By aligning IT governance with enterprise governance, COBIT helps organizations ensure that IT resources and processes are aligned with organizational goals, strategies, and performance objectives. This alignment is essential for achieving long-term business success and ensuring that IT delivers maximum value to the business.

Another critical aspect of COBIT is its focus on stakeholder engagement and communication. Effective IT governance requires the active involvement of various stakeholders, including business leaders, IT professionals, and external partners. COBIT provides guidelines for engaging stakeholders in the governance process, ensuring that their perspectives and interests are taken into account when making decisions about IT investments, resource allocation, and risk management. This collaborative approach to governance ensures that IT decisions are aligned with business needs, and that all stakeholders have a clear understanding of the value and impact of IT within the organization.

In summary, the COBIT framework for IT governance and management is a powerful tool for organizations seeking to optimize their IT operations, manage risks, ensure compliance, and deliver value to the business. By providing a structured, comprehensive approach to IT governance, COBIT helps organizations align their IT resources with business objectives, improve performance, and mitigate risks. The framework's emphasis on transparency, accountability, and stakeholder engagement ensures that IT decisions are well-informed, strategically aligned, and effectively executed. As organizations continue to rely on technology to drive business success, COBIT provides a solid foundation for managing IT in a way that supports both short-term goals and long-term growth.

The Role of COBIT in ITSM

The relationship between COBIT (Control Objectives for Information and Related Technologies) and IT Service Management (ITSM) is a vital one, as COBIT provides the governance framework that complements ITSM's focus on the operational delivery of IT services. While ITSM is concerned with the processes and practices that govern how IT services are delivered to meet customer needs, COBIT offers a broader, enterprise-wide governance framework that ensures the organization's IT functions align with overall business goals and objectives. Together, COBIT and ITSM enable organizations to improve their IT operations, manage risks effectively, and deliver consistent, high-quality services to customers.

COBIT plays a crucial role in ensuring that ITSM is governed effectively across the organization. ITSM frameworks like ITIL (Information Technology Infrastructure Library) provide detailed best practices for managing services in a structured and efficient way. However, ITIL focuses more on the management and operational aspects of service delivery. COBIT, on the other hand, provides the overarching governance structure that ensures ITSM processes are aligned with the business strategy, comply with regulations, and operate effectively within the organization. By bridging the gap between business objectives and IT operations, COBIT helps organizations align their service management practices with the overall business goals, ensuring that IT services contribute to business success.

One of the key areas where COBIT and ITSM intersect is in the establishment of clear governance frameworks for IT services. ITSM focuses on service delivery processes, including incident management, problem management, and service level management, among others. COBIT ensures that these processes are not only operationally effective but also strategically aligned with the business. For example, COBIT's principles of strategic alignment and performance management help ensure that IT services are designed and delivered in a way that meets the needs of the business and delivers measurable value. By integrating these governance principles with ITSM processes, organizations can ensure that their service management practices contribute to business success, meet customer expectations, and deliver high-quality, reliable services.

COBIT's focus on performance management is particularly relevant to ITSM, as it helps organizations ensure that IT services meet established performance criteria and service levels. While ITSM processes such as service level management define service expectations and ensure services are delivered according to agreed-upon standards, COBIT provides the metrics and measures to monitor the effectiveness of these services at an organizational level. COBIT enables organizations to define key performance indicators (KPIs) for IT services, monitor their performance over time, and take corrective actions when service levels are not met. This alignment of performance management across ITSM and COBIT ensures that organizations can evaluate the success of their IT services and continuously improve them to meet evolving business needs.

Another key area where COBIT supports ITSM is in risk management. COBIT emphasizes the importance of identifying, assessing, and managing risks related to IT operations, including those associated with service delivery. ITSM processes, such as incident management and change management, are designed to minimize risks by quickly resolving service disruptions and ensuring that changes to IT systems are made in a controlled and predictable manner. COBIT complements these processes by providing a framework for assessing and managing risks at a broader, organizational level. This ensures that IT services not only meet operational requirements but are also delivered in a way that minimizes risk to the business, such as financial, security, and compliance risks. Through this governance lens, COBIT helps organizations identify and mitigate risks before they can negatively impact service delivery or business operations.

The integration of COBIT with ITSM also helps organizations establish and maintain compliance with industry regulations and standards. As organizations face increasing scrutiny from regulators, ensuring compliance with legal and regulatory requirements is critical to maintaining trust and avoiding legal consequences. ITSM processes focus on managing service delivery, but COBIT ensures that service management practices comply with relevant laws and industry standards, such as data privacy regulations, cybersecurity requirements, and financial reporting obligations. By aligning ITSM processes with COBIT's governance framework, organizations can ensure that their IT services meet regulatory requirements while also being aligned with business goals. COBIT helps establish processes that allow for continuous monitoring of compliance, ensuring that the organization's IT operations remain secure, ethical, and in line with both internal policies and external regulatory demands.

Furthermore, COBIT's emphasis on continuous improvement aligns perfectly with the continual service improvement (CSI) principle in ITSM. CSI encourages organizations to evaluate their services and processes regularly, identify areas for enhancement, and implement changes to improve service delivery. COBIT supports this by providing a structured approach to performance measurement, monitoring, and assessment. By using COBIT's principles of continual improvement, organizations can assess their ITSM processes, identify gaps or inefficiencies, and take corrective actions to improve their service management practices. This proactive approach to improvement ensures that IT services remain agile, adaptable, and capable of meeting the changing needs of the business and its customers.

COBIT also plays an important role in defining roles and responsibilities within the IT service management system. ITSM processes rely on clearly defined roles for service owners, service managers, and support teams, but COBIT helps ensure that these roles are integrated into the larger governance structure of the organization. It provides a framework for defining accountability at all levels of the organization, ensuring that responsibilities for managing IT services are clearly articulated, and performance is monitored. By aligning these roles with the overall governance structure, COBIT ensures that the delivery of IT services is well-managed, transparent, and accountable.

Another critical area where COBIT adds value to ITSM is in the integration of IT services with business strategy. ITSM processes are typically focused on managing the operational aspects of IT service delivery, such as service availability, incident resolution, and user support. COBIT ensures that these operational activities are aligned with the strategic goals of the organization. It encourages organizations to assess the impact of IT services on business outcomes, ensuring that the delivery of IT services supports business objectives. This strategic alignment ensures that IT investments are optimized, and resources are used effectively to drive business success. By fostering this alignment, COBIT ensures that IT is not seen as a cost center but as a strategic enabler of business goals.

Finally, the integration of COBIT and ITSM facilitates better decision-making at all levels of the organization. COBIT provides a structured governance framework that ensures that IT service management processes are aligned with business needs, while ITSM ensures that IT services are delivered efficiently and effectively. Together, these frameworks enable organizations to make informed decisions about IT investments, service improvements, and resource allocation, leading to better service delivery and greater business success. By using both COBIT and ITSM together, organizations can ensure that their IT operations are optimized, risks are mitigated, and customer satisfaction is improved, leading to long-term business growth and success.

In summary, COBIT plays a vital role in ITSM by providing a comprehensive governance framework that ensures IT services are aligned with business goals, performance is monitored, risks are managed, and compliance is maintained. While ITSM focuses on service delivery, COBIT ensures that these services are governed effectively and strategically, leading to improved decision-making, better service quality, and enhanced business outcomes. Through their complementary roles, COBIT and ITSM enable organizations to deliver high-quality IT services that meet customer expectations, comply with regulatory requirements, and support long-term business success.

ITSM with Lean Methodology

The integration of Lean methodology with IT Service Management (ITSM) is a powerful approach that allows organizations to optimize their service delivery while reducing waste and increasing efficiency. Lean, originally developed in the manufacturing sector to streamline production processes, focuses on maximizing value by eliminating waste, improving flow, and empowering teams to continuously improve their processes. When applied to ITSM, Lean principles aim to enhance the efficiency and effectiveness of IT service delivery, ultimately leading to improved customer satisfaction and better alignment with business goals.

At the core of Lean methodology is the concept of value, which is defined as any action or service that contributes to meeting customer needs and expectations. In the context of ITSM, value is derived from the IT services that are delivered to users and customers. Lean encourages organizations to focus on delivering value by identifying and eliminating any activities, processes, or steps that do not directly contribute to meeting customer needs. This is done through the identification and elimination of waste, which is defined as any activity or resource that consumes time, effort, or resources without adding value to the customer. By applying Lean principles to ITSM, organizations can streamline their service management processes, reduce unnecessary complexity, and improve the overall quality of their IT services.

One of the key principles of Lean is continuous improvement, which is a fundamental aspect of ITSM as well. In traditional IT service management frameworks like ITIL, continual service improvement (CSI) is a critical element that focuses on evaluating service performance, identifying areas for improvement, and implementing changes to enhance the quality of IT services. Lean methodology enhances this approach by emphasizing a culture of ongoing improvement at all levels of the organization. Lean encourages ITSM teams to engage in regular reflection and assessment of their processes to identify opportunities for improvement. Through small, incremental changes and the continuous optimization of processes, Lean helps organizations reduce inefficiencies and enhance service delivery over time.

Another central Lean principle that complements ITSM is the focus on process flow. In ITSM, service delivery often involves multiple steps, from incident resolution and change management to problem management and service request fulfillment. These processes can become fragmented, slow, and prone to delays if not properly managed. Lean methodology focuses on improving flow by eliminating bottlenecks and ensuring that work moves efficiently through the system without unnecessary delays or interruptions. In the context of ITSM, this means streamlining service management processes to ensure that incidents are resolved quickly, changes are implemented with minimal disruption, and service requests are fulfilled promptly. By optimizing the flow of work, organizations can provide faster, more reliable IT services that meet customer expectations and business requirements.

Lean also emphasizes the importance of empowering employees and fostering a culture of collaboration and ownership. In ITSM, this translates into empowering service desk agents, incident managers, change managers, and other IT staff to take ownership of their processes and make decisions that improve service delivery. Lean encourages organizations to involve front-line employees in identifying inefficiencies and proposing solutions to improve processes. By involving those who are closest to the work in decision-making, Lean creates a sense of ownership and accountability, which leads to more engaged employees and better service outcomes. In the context of ITSM, this might involve allowing service desk agents to resolve issues without escalating them unnecessarily or enabling teams to quickly implement process improvements based on their daily experiences.

The application of Lean methodology to ITSM also focuses on reducing cycle time, which refers to the amount of time it takes to complete a particular task or process. In ITSM, this could mean reducing the time it takes to resolve incidents, process changes, or fulfill service requests. Lean emphasizes the need to streamline workflows and remove non-value-added activities that slow down the process. For example, in incident management, Lean might focus on reducing the number of steps needed to classify, assign, and resolve incidents, thereby speeding up the resolution time and reducing the impact of service disruptions. In change management, Lean can help minimize delays caused by unnecessary approvals or redundant checks, ensuring that changes are implemented quickly and with minimal disruption.

One of the most significant benefits of applying Lean to ITSM is the improvement in resource utilization. ITSM processes often involve a considerable amount of time and resources, especially in large organizations with complex IT environments. Lean helps organizations make better use of their resources by eliminating waste and ensuring that staff, technology, and other resources are used efficiently. This could mean reducing the time spent on repetitive administrative tasks, automating routine processes, or reallocating resources to higher-priority activities. By improving resource utilization, organizations can achieve more with fewer resources, leading to cost savings and more effective service delivery.

Lean's focus on customer value also aligns well with ITSM's goal of enhancing customer satisfaction. By eliminating waste and optimizing service delivery processes, organizations can provide faster, more reliable, and higher-quality services to customers. This focus on customer value is particularly important in IT service management, where the quality and timeliness of service delivery can directly impact user productivity and business operations. Lean encourages ITSM teams to continuously assess the needs and expectations of customers, ensuring that services are delivered in a way that provides maximum value. This customer-centric approach fosters stronger relationships with end-users and enhances overall satisfaction with IT services.

Moreover, Lean helps create a more transparent and accountable IT service management environment. By mapping out processes, identifying waste, and tracking performance, Lean provides organizations with a clear view of how services are delivered and where improvements are needed. This transparency enables organizations to make data-driven decisions and track progress over time. In ITSM, this could involve using Lean tools like value stream mapping and Kaizen events to visualize workflows, identify inefficiencies, and implement process improvements. By providing a clear picture of service delivery, Lean helps organizations make informed decisions that drive better outcomes for both the business and its customers.

The integration of Lean with ITSM also enhances the organization's ability to adapt to changing business requirements and customer needs. In today's fast-paced business environment, organizations need to be agile and responsive to shifting demands. Lean's emphasis on continuous improvement and process flexibility helps organizations quickly adapt their IT service management practices to meet these evolving needs. Whether it's responding to changes in technology, business priorities, or customer expectations, Lean ensures that IT services can be adjusted quickly and efficiently to stay aligned with the organization's goals.

Ultimately, the integration of Lean methodology with ITSM provides organizations with a comprehensive approach to optimizing their IT service delivery. By focusing on eliminating waste, improving flow, and continuously improving processes, Lean enhances the effectiveness of ITSM practices, leading to faster, more reliable, and cost-effective services. This approach enables organizations to not only meet but exceed customer expectations, driving both operational efficiency and business success. The Lean-ITSM combination empowers organizations to continuously evolve their IT services, ensuring that they remain responsive to the dynamic needs of the business and the customers they serve.

ITSM with Agile Methodology

The integration of Agile methodology with IT Service Management (ITSM) presents a dynamic approach to enhancing the flexibility, efficiency, and responsiveness of IT services. Agile, originally developed for software development, focuses on iterative progress, collaboration, flexibility, and customer feedback. When applied to ITSM, Agile principles aim to improve the speed, quality, and adaptability of IT services while maintaining alignment with business objectives. This combination fosters a culture of continuous improvement, customer-centric service delivery, and proactive service management that is better able to meet the rapidly changing demands of modern business environments.

The Agile methodology's emphasis on flexibility and adaptability makes it particularly well-suited for ITSM. In traditional ITSM frameworks such as ITIL, service management processes are often seen as structured and predefined, which can sometimes lead to slow response times and rigidity in addressing changing business requirements. Agile disrupts this by promoting shorter feedback loops, continuous delivery, and flexibility in the way services are designed, delivered, and improved. With Agile, IT service teams can more quickly respond to changes, whether they come from business demands, new technologies, or customer expectations. This allows ITSM to be more adaptive, ensuring that services are not only reactive but proactively adjusted to better meet organizational needs.

One of the primary advantages of using Agile within ITSM is its focus on continuous improvement. Agile projects are typically broken into small, manageable increments or sprints, each with its own set of deliverables. This incremental approach allows IT service teams to release updates, fixes, or improvements to services more regularly, providing immediate value to customers and stakeholders. By breaking down complex service management processes into smaller, manageable pieces, Agile enables organizations to quickly implement improvements without waiting for lengthy approval cycles or project completions. This ability to adapt quickly and iterate on service delivery results in faster resolution times, improved user experiences, and more effective service management processes.

Agile also places a strong emphasis on collaboration, both within IT teams and with other departments and stakeholders. In an ITSM context, collaboration is essential for ensuring that service management processes align with business needs. Agile methodologies, such as Scrum or Kanban, provide frameworks that encourage daily meetings, feedback, and shared responsibility. These practices ensure that service teams are continually communicating and working together toward common goals. For example, during an incident management process, Agile teams can collaborate in real-time to resolve issues quickly, constantly improving the process based on feedback and lessons learned from previous incidents. This collaborative approach fosters transparency and alignment between IT teams and business units, creating stronger relationships and improving service delivery outcomes.

Another key principle of Agile is customer collaboration over contract negotiation, which aligns well with ITSM's focus on customer satisfaction. Agile methodologies prioritize the needs and feedback of end-users, ensuring that services are developed with the customer in mind and refined based on ongoing input. ITSM, when combined with Agile, allows service teams to continuously engage with customers to understand their pain points, preferences, and expectations. This close collaboration results in services that are more attuned to the needs of users, leading to higher levels of satisfaction and more efficient service delivery. Agile's iterative approach also means that services can evolve as customer needs change, ensuring that IT services are always relevant and valuable.

One of the core concepts of Agile, particularly in Scrum, is the concept of user stories. User stories are short, simple descriptions of features or tasks from the perspective of the end user. In ITSM, adopting user stories allows IT service teams to frame issues, improvements, and new features in terms of customer needs. For example, rather than focusing solely on technical details, an IT service team might prioritize a user story that focuses on resolving a recurring issue for end-users, such as reducing downtime or improving the performance of a critical service. This user-centered approach helps ensure that the service management process is always aligned with the business and customer objectives, making it more outcome-driven and value-oriented.

Moreover, Agile practices within ITSM can help organizations improve their ability to manage changes efficiently. Change management, often a complex and bureaucratic process in traditional ITSM, can be more fluid and responsive when using Agile principles. With Agile, the change process becomes more iterative, with smaller, less disruptive changes being implemented more frequently. This reduces the risk associated with large, one-time changes and allows IT teams to address immediate issues or improvements quickly. Agile methods also emphasize minimizing waste and unnecessary steps, which is beneficial in streamlining the change management process. By applying Agile to change management, organizations can enhance the speed of service delivery, reduce the impact of changes on end-users, and improve the overall effectiveness of IT operations.

Another area where Agile complements ITSM is in the use of metrics and data. Agile encourages the use of key performance indicators (KPIs) to track the success of each iteration and guide continuous improvement. Similarly, ITSM processes require the monitoring of service performance, user satisfaction, and other metrics to evaluate the effectiveness of service delivery. By integrating Agile's focus on data-driven decision-making with ITSM's service performance metrics, organizations can create a feedback loop that continuously informs the refinement of services. These metrics help IT teams track progress, identify areas for improvement, and validate whether the desired outcomes are being achieved. This data-driven approach enables organizations to make more informed decisions about their IT services and adjust service delivery based on real-time insights.

The Agile approach also helps organizations better manage their service delivery capacity. ITSM processes often require balancing resources across multiple services, incidents, and requests. Agile's iterative approach and focus on delivering small, manageable increments of work allow IT service teams to prioritize tasks more effectively, ensuring that they are addressing the most critical issues first. Agile practices such as Kanban or Scrum also help in visualizing work, allowing teams to track service requests and workloads, identify bottlenecks, and ensure that resources are allocated efficiently. This improved visibility and flexibility in managing workloads leads to faster resolution times and better service delivery.

The collaborative, customer-centric, and iterative nature of Agile provides ITSM teams with a framework that allows them to continuously adapt and improve their service delivery. Agile practices encourage IT teams to work closely with business units, focus on customer needs, and iterate rapidly based on feedback. This approach fosters greater innovation and agility in IT service delivery, which is crucial in an environment where customer expectations are constantly evolving, and technology is rapidly changing. ITSM, when combined with Agile, becomes a more dynamic, responsive, and customer-oriented framework, ensuring that IT services remain effective, relevant, and aligned with the business's goals.

Incorporating Agile into ITSM not only enhances the speed and efficiency of service delivery but also ensures that IT services are continuously improved and refined based on real-world feedback. By embracing Agile's principles of flexibility, collaboration, and customer focus, ITSM teams can enhance their ability to meet business needs, improve service quality, and achieve higher levels of customer satisfaction. The Agile methodology's emphasis on rapid iterations, flexibility in the face of change, and customer collaboration ensures that IT services remain adaptable, effective, and always aligned with organizational goals. Through this synergy, organizations can create IT service management practices that are both efficient and responsive to the demands of modern business environments.

ITSM with DevOps

The integration of IT Service Management (ITSM) with DevOps presents a transformative approach to how IT services are delivered and managed, enabling organizations to bridge the gap between development and operations teams. ITSM is focused on the management and delivery of IT services that align with business needs, while DevOps emphasizes collaboration, automation, and continuous delivery of high-quality software. Combining these two frameworks allows organizations to achieve a more agile, efficient, and responsive approach to service delivery that can rapidly adapt to changing business requirements. This integration facilitates not only improved service delivery but also better alignment between IT operations and software development, ultimately contributing to the success of the organization.

At its core, DevOps is about collaboration between development and IT operations teams, with a strong focus on automation, continuous integration, continuous delivery, and monitoring. The goal is to enable faster and more reliable software deployment while maintaining high standards of service quality. ITSM, traditionally concerned with processes such as incident management, change management, and service level management, provides a structured framework for managing the IT services that support business operations. When combined, DevOps and ITSM complement each other by fostering collaboration and agility, ensuring that IT services are delivered efficiently, reliably, and in alignment with customer needs.

The collaboration between ITSM and DevOps becomes particularly important in today's fast-paced business environment, where organizations must be able to respond quickly to market changes and customer demands. By adopting both frameworks, organizations can improve the speed of software delivery while ensuring that IT services are continuously monitored, controlled, and optimized to meet business needs. DevOps practices such as continuous integration and continuous delivery (CI/CD) allow development teams to release software updates quickly and frequently. However, without the structured processes provided by ITSM, such as change management and incident management, this speed could introduce risks, such as service disruptions or poor-quality releases. By integrating DevOps with ITSM, organizations can manage these risks effectively while maintaining the agility needed to stay competitive.

Change management, a critical process within ITSM, plays an essential role in the integration with DevOps. In a traditional IT environment, change management processes can be slow and cumbersome, creating bottlenecks that hinder the speed of service delivery. However, DevOps emphasizes the need for continuous change and rapid iterations. By applying ITSM's change management processes in the context of DevOps, organizations can ensure that changes are introduced in a controlled, predictable manner, even in an environment characterized by frequent releases and updates. This integration allows for a balance between speed and control, ensuring that software updates and changes are deployed efficiently while minimizing disruptions to production systems.

Incident management, another key ITSM process, is equally important in a DevOps environment. DevOps promotes the idea of continuously monitoring and improving software, but when issues arise in production, rapid resolution is essential to avoid service disruptions. ITSM's incident management processes provide the structured approach necessary to quickly identify, diagnose, and resolve incidents. Integrating incident management with DevOps enables organizations to respond to issues in real-time, ensuring that incidents are dealt with swiftly and efficiently. Furthermore, DevOps practices such as automated testing and monitoring can help reduce the frequency and severity of incidents by proactively identifying potential issues before they impact users.

One of the most significant benefits of combining ITSM with DevOps is the improvement in service quality. ITSM's focus on service level management ensures that IT services meet agreed-upon performance levels and customer expectations. By integrating DevOps practices such as automated testing and continuous delivery with ITSM's service level management processes, organizations can ensure that software releases are not only frequent but also of high quality. Continuous testing and automated deployment pipelines allow development teams to catch issues early in the development cycle, leading to fewer defects and a higher-quality product being delivered to end-users. ITSM's service monitoring and performance management processes complement this by tracking the performance of services in real-time, allowing organizations to identify and resolve issues quickly.

Furthermore, the integration of ITSM with DevOps enables a more comprehensive approach to managing IT resources. DevOps encourages the use of infrastructure as code (IaC), automation, and cloud technologies to streamline the development and deployment of software. ITSM processes ensure that these technologies are deployed in a controlled and efficient manner, ensuring compliance with organizational standards and policies. By combining DevOps' focus on automation and speed with ITSM's emphasis on governance and control, organizations can maintain a well-managed and secure IT environment while delivering services rapidly.

The collaborative nature of DevOps also enhances ITSM's effectiveness. In traditional ITSM environments, IT teams often work in silos, with development, operations, and service management teams operating independently. DevOps, however, encourages cross-functional collaboration, ensuring that all stakeholders are involved in the software delivery process. This collaborative approach not only enhances the speed and quality of software delivery but also improves the communication between teams responsible for IT service management. By breaking down the barriers between development, operations, and service management, organizations can create a more cohesive and efficient service delivery process that meets business goals and customer expectations.

As organizations adopt Agile methodologies in development, the need for faster, more flexible service management practices becomes more pronounced. ITSM frameworks, which have traditionally been seen as rigid, can be adapted to complement Agile principles by incorporating flexibility and iterative processes. In this environment, DevOps' focus on continuous integration and continuous delivery works hand-in-hand with ITSM's structured service management practices to ensure that the delivery of services is both agile and controlled. By using Agile and DevOps principles within ITSM, organizations can create a more responsive IT environment that can quickly adjust to changing business needs and market conditions.

Finally, the integration of DevOps with ITSM leads to a more sustainable and resilient IT service delivery model. Through automation, continuous monitoring, and collaborative practices, DevOps helps organizations build more robust and scalable systems. ITSM, with its focus on risk management, service quality, and continuous improvement, ensures that these systems are not only efficient but also secure, compliant, and aligned with business objectives. This combination of agility, collaboration, and structured service management allows organizations to deliver IT services that are not only fast and responsive but also reliable, secure, and sustainable over the long term.

By integrating ITSM with DevOps, organizations can create a service delivery environment that is both agile and governed. This integration allows for rapid software delivery while maintaining the necessary controls and oversight to ensure that services meet quality standards and business objectives. The combination of DevOps' speed and ITSM's structure leads to improved service quality, reduced risk, and better alignment with business goals. In an increasingly competitive and dynamic market, this integrated approach enables organizations to respond quickly to customer needs, drive innovation, and maintain a high level of service excellence.

The Role of the Service Desk in ITSM

The service desk is often considered the cornerstone of IT Service Management (ITSM), serving as the primary point of contact between IT services and end-users. It is the central hub for handling incidents, service requests, and general IT-related inquiries. The service desk plays a crucial role in ensuring the smooth functioning of IT services, supporting users, and maintaining communication between IT departments and customers. As organizations increasingly rely on technology for their daily operations, the service desk's role in ITSM has become more critical than ever, not only in resolving issues but also in enhancing the overall user experience and supporting the strategic goals of the organization.

The primary function of the service desk within ITSM is incident management, which involves the resolution of disruptions to IT services that affect users and business operations. When a user encounters an issue with an IT service, the service desk serves as the first point of contact to report and address the problem. By efficiently categorizing, prioritizing, and resolving incidents, the service desk helps minimize downtime and ensures that users can quickly resume their work with minimal disruption. The importance of incident management cannot be overstated, as service disruptions, no matter how small, can have significant consequences for productivity and business continuity. By providing quick and efficient incident resolution, the service desk supports organizational resilience and ensures that IT services are always available when needed.

In addition to incident management, the service desk is responsible for managing service requests, which are formalized user inquiries or requests for standard IT services, such as software installations, password resets, or access to specific applications. While incidents are typically unplanned disruptions, service requests are generally routine tasks that need to be processed and fulfilled in a standardized manner. The service desk acts as the interface between users and IT, ensuring that service requests are handled in accordance with defined service level agreements (SLAs). By efficiently managing service requests, the service desk ensures that users receive timely and consistent support, enhancing their overall satisfaction with IT services.

The service desk's role in ITSM extends beyond simply resolving incidents and fulfilling service requests. It also involves proactive support and communication. Service desk agents are often the first to receive feedback from end-users, providing them with valuable insights into the usability and performance of IT services. By collecting and analyzing feedback, the service desk can identify recurring issues, areas for improvement, and opportunities to optimize service delivery. This proactive approach enables the service desk to anticipate potential problems, implement preventive measures, and continuously improve the quality of service provided to users. Additionally, the service desk can serve as a communication channel between IT and business stakeholders, ensuring that users are kept informed about the status of ongoing incidents, changes, or updates to IT services.

One of the key aspects of the service desk's role in ITSM is its alignment with the broader objectives of IT governance. The service desk is not just a reactive entity that resolves issues as they arise; it also plays a key role in ensuring that IT services are aligned with the business needs and objectives. By adhering to ITSM best practices, such as those outlined in frameworks like ITIL, the service desk ensures that incidents and service requests are handled in a way that supports the organization's strategic goals. This alignment is crucial, as it ensures that the IT department is not just managing technology, but is actively contributing to the business's success by delivering services that support its operations, growth, and customer satisfaction.

Service desks in ITSM are also tasked with handling change management processes. While the primary responsibility for change management lies with the change management team, the service desk plays an essential role in communicating planned changes, potential disruptions, and service outages to end-users. Effective communication is vital to managing change, as it helps to prepare users for any temporary disruptions or changes to their workflows. The service desk serves as the communication link between IT and users, ensuring that users are aware of scheduled maintenance, updates, or changes to IT services. This role is crucial in managing user expectations and minimizing resistance to change.

Furthermore, the service desk is responsible for maintaining a comprehensive knowledge base that helps to enhance the efficiency of IT service delivery. By documenting known issues, solutions, and workarounds, the service desk creates a valuable resource that can be used by both IT staff and end-users. A well-maintained knowledge base allows service desk agents to resolve issues more quickly by providing them with the information they need to troubleshoot problems efficiently. Additionally, users can access the knowledge base to find solutions to common issues without needing to contact the service desk, which improves self-service capabilities and reduces the workload on service desk agents. The knowledge base is an essential tool for improving both the speed and quality of IT support.

The role of the service desk in ITSM also includes monitoring and tracking the performance of IT services. By tracking key performance indicators (KPIs) such as incident resolution times, service request fulfillment rates, and customer satisfaction scores, the service desk provides valuable insights into the effectiveness of IT service delivery. This data can be used to assess whether service levels are being met, identify areas for improvement, and measure the overall performance of IT services. By monitoring and reporting on service desk performance, organizations can ensure that IT services are consistently meeting business and user needs, and can take corrective action when necessary.

Service desks are also critical in driving a culture of continual improvement within ITSM. By constantly evaluating service delivery, tracking performance, and gathering feedback from users, the service desk helps identify opportunities for process improvements. This ongoing evaluation allows IT teams to refine their practices, enhance service delivery, and reduce inefficiencies over time. The service desk's involvement in continual improvement also ensures that IT services remain responsive to changing business needs and evolving technologies, allowing organizations to stay competitive in a rapidly changing market.

Finally, the service desk plays an integral role in customer satisfaction and user experience. As the first point of contact for users experiencing IT issues, the service desk directly influences how users perceive IT services and the overall IT department. A well-managed, responsive, and user-friendly service desk enhances the overall experience for end-users, creating a positive impression of IT services within the organization. High-quality service desk support can foster greater user trust, loyalty, and satisfaction, which ultimately contributes to the success of the organization. In contrast, poor service desk performance can lead to frustration, decreased productivity, and dissatisfaction with IT services.

The service desk, as a critical component of ITSM, is much more than a reactive support function. It plays a proactive, strategic role in ensuring that IT services are delivered efficiently, meet user needs, and align with business objectives. By managing incidents and service requests, supporting change management processes, maintaining a knowledge base, and driving continual improvement, the service desk enhances the overall effectiveness of IT service management. It serves as the interface between IT and the rest of the organization, ensuring that users receive the support they need to perform their work effectively while also contributing to the ongoing optimization of IT services. The service desk's ability to foster collaboration, communication, and continuous improvement makes it a central pillar of ITSM and an essential enabler of business success.

Service Management Tools and Technologies

Service management tools and technologies play a pivotal role in the effective delivery of IT services. These tools are designed to help organizations automate, streamline, and optimize their service management processes, ensuring that IT services are delivered efficiently, consistently, and in alignment with business goals. With the increasing complexity of IT environments and the growing demands for faster, more reliable services, service management tools have become an indispensable part of modern IT Service Management (ITSM) frameworks. These tools provide organizations with the necessary capabilities to manage incidents, changes, service requests, configurations, and performance metrics, among other critical IT operations.

One of the primary functions of service management tools is to support incident management. Incidents are any disruptions or degradations of IT services, and resolving them quickly is critical to maintaining service continuity and minimizing the impact on end-users and business operations. Service management tools provide IT teams with centralized platforms to track, prioritize, and resolve incidents. Through automated workflows, incident tickets can be logged, assigned to appropriate teams, and tracked until they are resolved. These tools enable incident response teams to manage large volumes of incidents effectively, ensuring that the most critical issues are addressed first and that no incident is left unaddressed. They also help capture valuable data that can be used for analysis, identifying trends, and preventing future incidents.

Change management is another area where service management tools play a crucial role. Managing changes in an IT environment can be complex, especially when multiple systems, applications, and stakeholders are involved. Service management tools enable organizations to automate and streamline the change management process, ensuring that changes are properly planned, tested, and implemented with minimal disruption to business operations. These tools help in managing change requests, assessing risks, and tracking approvals, all while maintaining detailed records of the changes made.

This centralized approach reduces the risk of errors, improves the visibility of changes, and ensures that all changes align with organizational policies and service level agreements (SLAs).

Service management tools also provide robust capabilities for managing service requests, which are typically routine tasks or user requests such as software installations, password resets, or access to applications. These tools offer self-service portals that allow users to submit requests and track their progress in real-time. By automating the handling of service requests, organizations can reduce the workload of service desk agents and enable quicker resolution times. Additionally, service management tools enable IT teams to standardize service request workflows, ensuring consistency and efficiency in service delivery. With the help of these tools, organizations can provide a more seamless and responsive user experience, improving overall customer satisfaction.

Configuration management is another critical function supported by service management tools. Configuration management involves maintaining an up-to-date record of all IT assets, including hardware, software, and network configurations. Service management tools, such as configuration management databases (CMDBs), provide organizations with a centralized repository to track and manage these assets. By maintaining accurate and detailed records of IT configurations, organizations can ensure better control over their IT environment, improve decision-making, and minimize the risk of configuration errors. Service management tools also support the visualization of relationships between different IT assets, making it easier to identify potential issues and dependencies that could affect service delivery.

In addition to managing incidents, changes, and service requests, service management tools play a critical role in monitoring and reporting on service performance. Performance management tools enable organizations to track key performance indicators (KPIs), measure service levels, and monitor system health in real-time. By providing visibility into the performance of IT services, these tools help IT teams proactively identify issues before they impact users. Service management tools also allow organizations to generate detailed reports that provide insights into service delivery, helping management make informed decisions and prioritize improvements. The integration of monitoring tools with ITSM systems helps in identifying performance bottlenecks, service interruptions, or areas where service levels are not being met, allowing for corrective actions to be taken promptly.

Automation is one of the most significant benefits that service management tools bring to ITSM. By automating repetitive and manual tasks, service management tools reduce the administrative burden on IT staff, allowing them to focus on more complex and value-added activities. For example, service management tools can automate incident routing, ticket escalation, and notifications, ensuring that the right people are informed at the right time. They can also automate the process of applying patches, updating software, and resolving simple issues, reducing response times and improving overall efficiency. The use of automation not only speeds up the service management process but also ensures consistency and accuracy in task execution, reducing the likelihood of human error.

Another important aspect of service management tools is their ability to integrate with other IT systems and business applications. Integration with monitoring tools, customer relationship management (CRM) systems, enterprise resource planning (ERP) systems, and other enterprise tools allows for the seamless exchange of information and a more comprehensive view of IT operations. For example, integrating service management tools with monitoring systems allows IT teams to correlate incident data with system alerts, providing a clearer understanding of the root cause of issues. Integration with CRM systems helps provide context about users or customers submitting service requests, enabling more personalized and efficient service delivery. These integrations improve the overall workflow and ensure that IT service management is aligned with broader organizational processes.

The evolution of cloud computing has also influenced the development and deployment of service management tools. Cloud-based service management platforms offer significant advantages over traditional on-premise solutions, including scalability, flexibility, and cost-effectiveness. Cloud-based tools enable organizations to easily scale their service management operations as their business grows, without the need for significant infrastructure investments. These tools are also accessible from anywhere, allowing IT teams to manage and monitor services remotely, which is particularly valuable in today's increasingly distributed work environments. Additionally, cloud-based service management tools often include built-in analytics and reporting features, providing organizations with real-time insights into service performance and user satisfaction.

Service management tools also contribute to improving IT governance and compliance. In regulated industries, organizations must adhere to strict compliance standards regarding data security, privacy, and reporting. Service management tools help organizations maintain compliance by providing the necessary documentation, audit trails, and reporting capabilities. For example, change management processes can be tracked and documented to ensure that all changes are properly authorized and comply with internal policies and regulatory requirements. By automating these processes and maintaining accurate records, service management tools help organizations mitigate the risk of non-compliance and ensure that they meet legal and regulatory obligations.

The integration of artificial intelligence (AI) and machine learning (ML) into service management tools is also becoming more prevalent. AI-powered service management tools can assist in incident resolution by automating responses to common issues and providing agents with intelligent recommendations based on past incidents and solutions. ML algorithms can analyze historical data to predict future incidents, identify trends, and recommend improvements to service delivery. By leveraging AI and ML, organizations can further enhance the efficiency and effectiveness of their service management processes, providing faster and more accurate resolutions to users and improving overall service quality.

In summary, service management tools and technologies are indispensable to the efficient delivery of IT services. They streamline processes, improve performance monitoring, enhance collaboration, and enable organizations to manage incidents, changes, service requests, and performance metrics effectively. By integrating automation, AI, and cloud-based solutions, service management tools continue to evolve, offering organizations the flexibility, scalability, and efficiency needed to meet the demands of modern IT environments. Through the adoption of these tools, organizations can improve their ITSM processes, deliver higher-quality services, and better align their IT operations with business goals.

Service Level Management in ITSM

Service Level Management (SLM) is a critical process within IT Service Management (ITSM) that ensures IT services meet the agreed-upon expectations and performance standards as defined in service level agreements (SLAs). It serves as the foundation for delivering consistent and reliable services to customers and stakeholders, aligning IT service delivery with business needs. By managing and monitoring service levels, SLM helps organizations meet the expectations of both internal and external customers while optimizing service delivery to achieve the highest possible levels of satisfaction and business value.

The role of Service Level Management in ITSM is multi-faceted, involving the creation, negotiation, and management of SLAs, as well as the continual monitoring and reporting of service performance against these agreements. SLAs are formal documents that outline the expected service levels for a particular service, such as uptime, response times, and issue resolution timeframes. These agreements are developed in collaboration with customers and stakeholders to ensure that both parties have a clear understanding of the service expectations, what is included in the service, and how performance will be measured. The creation of SLAs is one of the first steps in establishing a service management framework and is crucial for ensuring that IT services are aligned with business objectives and customer needs.

One of the primary functions of SLM is to define the specific metrics and key performance indicators (KPIs) that will be used to measure the performance of IT services. These metrics are typically based on the expectations set out in the SLA and are used to monitor service delivery, track progress, and ensure that services meet the required standards. Examples of service level metrics include system uptime, response times to incidents, the time taken to resolve service requests, and customer satisfaction levels. By setting clear metrics and performance indicators, SLM provides both IT teams and customers with a common understanding of what constitutes acceptable service levels and performance. Monitoring these metrics over time enables organizations to assess whether the services are being delivered as promised and provides valuable insights into areas where improvements may be needed.

An essential aspect of Service Level Management is the continual review and refinement of SLAs to ensure that they remain relevant and reflect changing business needs, technological advancements, and evolving customer expectations. Service delivery is dynamic, and as organizations grow, expand, or change their operations, the services they rely on must evolve as well. SLM ensures that SLAs are regularly reviewed, updated, and renegotiated, if necessary, to reflect these changes. For instance, if new business requirements emerge, such as the need for higher availability or faster response times, the SLA should be updated to reflect these updated expectations. SLM ensures that the service agreements are flexible enough to accommodate changes while maintaining alignment with both customer expectations and business objectives.

In addition to managing SLAs, Service Level Management is also responsible for managing the relationships between IT and its customers or stakeholders. It acts as a bridge between business needs and IT service delivery, ensuring that the services provided by the IT department support the strategic goals of the organization. This involves regular communication with customers, both internal and external, to understand their needs, expectations, and priorities. By maintaining open and transparent communication, SLM helps build trust and ensures that any issues or concerns regarding service levels are addressed proactively. It also helps to avoid misunderstandings by setting realistic and achievable service expectations from the outset.

One of the key challenges in Service Level Management is balancing the expectations of customers with the capabilities of IT. Often, customers may expect high levels of service performance, such as 100% uptime or immediate resolution of incidents. However, it is essential that the IT department manage these expectations realistically and ensure that the service levels specified in the SLA are both achievable and sustainable. SLM plays a critical role in this process by negotiating SLAs that are not only aligned with business requirements but also take into account the limitations of available resources and technology. It is important for IT teams to ensure that service level commitments are realistic and can be consistently met without placing undue strain on the organization's resources.

Service Level Management is also a key component in the overall performance and quality management of IT services. Through regular monitoring and reporting, SLM provides data and insights into how well services are being delivered and whether they are meeting the agreed-upon targets. This data can then be used to identify areas for improvement and inform decision-making for resource allocation, process optimization, and overall service management. The ongoing analysis of service performance also helps to identify trends or recurring issues that could indicate underlying problems within the IT environment, such as poor infrastructure performance, staffing shortages, or recurring technical issues. By addressing these issues and continuously improving service performance, SLM helps ensure that services remain reliable, efficient, and aligned with business goals.

A crucial element of Service Level Management is the relationship it has with other ITSM processes. SLM does not operate in isolation; instead, it is closely linked with processes such as incident management, problem management, and change management. For example, incident management plays a direct role in meeting SLA requirements by ensuring that incidents are logged, prioritized, and resolved within the agreed-upon timeframes. Problem management, on the other hand, helps to identify and resolve the root causes of recurring incidents, thus improving service reliability and reducing the likelihood of SLA breaches. By working in tandem with these other processes, Service Level Management ensures that the overall service delivery is efficient, effective, and consistent with the service level agreements.

Service Level Management also plays a key role in driving continual improvement within IT services. By regularly assessing service performance against SLA targets and using this data to drive improvements, SLM ensures that IT services evolve to meet changing business needs. This continuous cycle of review, feedback, and improvement aligns closely with the principles of continual service improvement (CSI) found in frameworks like ITIL. By identifying areas where service levels are not being met, SLM can help initiate corrective actions, implement process improvements, and ultimately enhance the quality of service delivery. This iterative improvement process ensures that services remain aligned with business needs and continue to provide value to customers over time.

In the context of ITSM, Service Level Management plays an indispensable role in aligning IT services with business objectives and customer expectations. It ensures that IT services are delivered according to agreed-upon standards, helping to build trust and satisfaction among customers. By defining clear service level metrics, managing relationships with stakeholders, and continuously improving service performance, SLM contributes to the overall efficiency, reliability, and success of IT service delivery. It also fosters a culture of accountability within the IT department, as performance against SLAs is regularly measured and reported, ensuring that the IT organization remains focused on meeting its commitments and delivering high-quality services. Through its proactive and continuous approach to managing service levels, SLM ensures that IT services not only meet current business needs but are also flexible enough to adapt to future challenges and opportunities.

Change Management in ITSM

Change management is a critical process within IT Service Management (ITSM) that helps organizations systematically plan, implement, and track changes to their IT services, infrastructure, and systems. Its primary objective is to minimize the impact of changes on service quality, system stability, and business operations. In a fast-paced, technology-driven environment, change management ensures that changes are made in a controlled and predictable manner, reducing risks and ensuring that IT services remain reliable, efficient, and aligned with business goals. Whether it's implementing a software update, deploying new hardware, or making adjustments to network configurations, change management plays an essential role in ensuring that all changes are planned, tested, and executed without disrupting business continuity.

The process of change management begins with a formal request for change (RFC), which is submitted when there is a need to modify an existing service or infrastructure. This request is carefully reviewed and evaluated to understand the potential impact, the resources required, and the risks associated with the proposed change. The evaluation process typically involves the participation of key stakeholders, including IT teams, business units, and, in some cases, external vendors or partners. The goal is to assess whether the change aligns with the organization's objectives, whether it will improve service delivery, and whether it can be implemented without causing significant disruption.

Once the RFC is reviewed, a change advisory board (CAB) is often involved in the decision-making process. The CAB is a group of individuals, including IT managers, project managers, and other relevant stakeholders, who evaluate the change request based on several criteria, including the potential impact on the business, the level of risk involved, and the resources required to implement the change. The CAB ensures that changes are not only necessary but also feasible within the organization's current capabilities. They also ensure that all potential risks have been identified and mitigated to prevent any unforeseen consequences.

After the change request is approved, change management involves detailed planning and preparation. This includes determining the timing of the change, how it will be communicated, and which resources will be allocated to ensure its successful implementation. In many cases, the change is implemented during scheduled maintenance windows or during off-peak hours to minimize the impact on users and business operations. The planning process also involves defining how the change will be tested before it is deployed to production, ensuring that any potential issues are identified and resolved in advance.

Testing is an essential part of the change management process, as it helps identify any unforeseen issues that might arise once the change is implemented. Testing ensures that the change meets the expected objectives without negatively impacting other systems or services. In complex IT environments, where changes can involve multiple systems, applications, and teams, thorough testing helps ensure that all components are working as expected. Furthermore, testing can reveal any compatibility issues between new and existing systems, preventing downtime or service disruptions once the change is live.

Once the change has been successfully implemented and tested, the change management process doesn't end there. A critical aspect of change management is post-implementation review and validation. After the change is deployed, the IT team continues to monitor the system to ensure that the desired outcomes are achieved and that no unforeseen issues have emerged. If problems arise, there are processes in place to quickly revert the change or apply fixes to restore service. Post-implementation reviews also provide valuable feedback for future changes, allowing the organization to continuously improve its change management practices. Lessons learned from previous changes are incorporated into future planning, creating a cycle of ongoing improvement.

A key benefit of change management is its ability to minimize the risk of service disruptions. In the absence of a formal change management process, changes to IT services are often made on an ad-hoc basis, increasing the likelihood of errors, service outages, and poor customer experiences. By implementing a structured process, organizations can ensure that changes are made in a controlled and predictable manner. This reduces the risk of unforeseen consequences, such as system downtime, data loss, or performance degradation. Change management helps maintain the stability of IT services, allowing businesses to deliver reliable services to their customers while also adapting to changing technological needs.

Change management also supports better communication across IT teams and with business stakeholders. By formalizing the process of submitting, reviewing, and implementing changes, change management provides a transparent framework for collaboration. IT teams are informed of upcoming changes, their potential impact, and the steps involved in their execution. Similarly, business stakeholders are kept informed of changes that may affect their operations, allowing them to prepare for any potential disruptions. This ensures that everyone involved is aligned and that expectations are properly managed throughout the change process.

Additionally, change management plays an important role in regulatory compliance and audit readiness. In industries where organizations must adhere to strict regulatory standards, such as healthcare, finance, or energy, change management ensures that all changes are properly documented, approved, and executed according to established policies. This provides a clear audit trail, which is essential for demonstrating compliance with industry regulations. By maintaining records of changes, including the rationale behind them, the steps taken to implement them, and any issues encountered, organizations can demonstrate that they are following best practices and meeting regulatory requirements.

Effective change management also promotes a culture of accountability and ownership within the IT department. Each change request is carefully tracked, and the individuals responsible for implementing the change are held accountable for its success. This accountability ensures that the necessary attention is given to every change, no matter how small. Furthermore, the change management process encourages IT teams to follow standardized procedures, ensuring that changes are executed with consistency and reliability. This contributes to a more organized and disciplined IT environment, where changes are made with careful planning and consideration.

The integration of change management with other ITSM processes is another important aspect of its success. Change management is closely linked with incident management, problem management, configuration management, and service level management. For example, changes to IT systems often arise as a result of incidents or problems, and incident management teams work closely with change management to ensure that any necessary fixes or improvements are implemented. Similarly, configuration management ensures that changes to IT assets are properly recorded and documented, allowing for greater visibility and control over the IT environment. By aligning change management with these other processes, organizations can create a seamless service management system that supports the efficient and reliable delivery of IT services.

In large, complex organizations, the change management process may be highly structured, with multiple levels of approval and detailed documentation. In smaller organizations or agile environments, change management may be more streamlined and flexible, with a focus on speed and efficiency. Regardless of the size or complexity of the organization, change management plays an essential role in ensuring that IT services are continuously improved while maintaining stability and minimizing risks. By effectively managing changes to IT services, organizations can support business growth, maintain high service quality, and meet customer expectations in an increasingly competitive and dynamic market.

Incident Management in ITSM

Incident Management is a core process within IT Service Management (ITSM) that focuses on restoring normal service operations as quickly as possible after an unplanned disruption or degradation. The main goal of Incident Management is to minimize the impact of incidents on business operations and to ensure that users experience minimal downtime. In today's highly digital business environment, where IT services are essential for almost every aspect of an organization's operations, a well-structured incident management process is crucial for maintaining service continuity and customer satisfaction. Effective Incident Management helps organizations respond quickly to issues, resolve them in a timely manner, and prevent service disruptions from escalating into more serious problems.

The process of Incident Management begins the moment an incident is reported, which can happen through various channels, such as user calls to the service desk, automated monitoring systems, or alerts from other IT teams. Once the incident is identified, it is logged and categorized by severity and impact. The severity of the incident determines how quickly it must be addressed, while the impact refers to the number of users or business operations affected by the disruption. Proper categorization of incidents is essential for ensuring that resources are allocated efficiently and that the right personnel are involved in resolving the issue.

Following the initial logging and categorization, the incident is prioritized based on its impact and urgency. High-priority incidents, such as those affecting critical business operations or a large number of users, are addressed first to ensure that the most critical services are restored as quickly as possible. Incident Management is designed to provide a structured approach to handling incidents, ensuring that the IT team addresses them in a systematic way that minimizes the potential for delays or mistakes. A well-structured process helps to ensure that incidents are resolved promptly and that users can return to their normal work with minimal disruption.

One of the key principles of Incident Management is to restore normal service operation as quickly as possible, even if a full resolution is not immediately available. In some cases, incidents may be resolved with a temporary workaround that allows users to continue working while a permanent fix is developed. This approach is often referred to as "fixing the symptom" rather than "the cause," which is a necessary step when the incident has to be addressed urgently. The temporary solution allows the IT team to buy time for a more comprehensive resolution while ensuring that business operations continue.

Once the incident has been resolved or a workaround has been implemented, the IT team must ensure that the incident is fully documented, including details of the root cause, steps taken to resolve the issue, and any lessons learned. Incident documentation is crucial not only for tracking the incident but also for future analysis. By reviewing incident reports, IT teams can identify trends, recurring issues, or areas where improvements are needed. Incident data can be analyzed to determine whether specific systems or processes are consistently causing disruptions, and this information can be used to improve system reliability and prevent similar incidents in the future.

Incident Management also plays a significant role in communication. Throughout the incident lifecycle, it is essential to keep stakeholders informed about the status of the incident and the progress being made toward resolution. Regular communication helps manage expectations, reduce frustration among users, and ensure that everyone involved in the resolution process is aligned. The service desk, acting as the central point of contact for users, plays a crucial role in managing this communication. Users need to be informed about the incident's status, estimated resolution time, and any workarounds that may be in place. Effective communication during an incident not only reduces user frustration but also helps maintain trust in IT services and the IT department.

One of the key challenges in Incident Management is balancing speed and quality. IT teams must work efficiently to resolve incidents quickly, but rushing to close tickets can lead to incomplete resolutions or missed underlying issues. While speed is important, the root cause of the incident must also be addressed to prevent future occurrences. Incident Management aims to strike a balance between delivering rapid solutions and ensuring that the underlying causes of incidents are thoroughly investigated and resolved. If incidents are repeatedly caused by the same underlying issue, it is critical that the IT team take the necessary steps to prevent the recurrence of that issue, which may involve further analysis or escalation to other processes like Problem Management.

Problem Management and Incident Management are closely linked, but they serve different purposes. While Incident Management focuses on restoring normal service operation as quickly as possible, Problem Management seeks to identify and eliminate the root causes of recurring incidents. If an incident is identified as being part of a broader trend or recurring issue, it may be escalated to Problem Management for further investigation. By working together, Incident Management and Problem Management ensure that IT services are not only restored quickly but that the underlying causes of disruptions are addressed to improve long-term service reliability.

In addition to dealing with internal incidents, Incident Management is also critical in dealing with external issues, such as those involving third-party vendors or service providers. When incidents are caused by external factors, such as a service interruption from an Internet Service Provider (ISP) or a third-party application, the Incident Management team must coordinate with external vendors to resolve the issue as quickly as possible. Effective communication between internal teams and external partners is key to ensuring a swift resolution and minimizing downtime. The service desk acts as the intermediary, ensuring that all relevant parties are informed and that the incident is tracked and resolved in a timely manner.

Service Level Agreements (SLAs) play an essential role in Incident Management. SLAs define the expected response and resolution times for incidents based on their severity and impact. These agreements set clear expectations between the IT department and the users, ensuring that both parties understand the timelines and priorities for incident resolution. Adhering to SLAs is crucial for maintaining user satisfaction and ensuring that the IT department meets its commitments. Incident Management helps to ensure that SLAs are consistently met by providing structured processes for incident handling and resolution. Regular reporting and analysis of SLA compliance can help identify areas for improvement and ensure that service delivery is continuously optimized.

Incident Management is also closely tied to the overall service improvement process within ITSM. As incidents are resolved, the data collected from each incident provides valuable insights into the performance of IT services and areas where improvements can be made. The lessons learned from incidents can be used to refine processes, enhance system reliability, and reduce the likelihood of future incidents. Incident data analysis can also reveal trends and recurring issues, allowing the IT department to proactively address problem areas before they result in significant disruptions. By integrating Incident Management with continuous service improvement initiatives, organizations can ensure that their IT services evolve and adapt to meet changing business needs and user expectations.

In large organizations with complex IT environments, Incident Management can be particularly challenging. However, when implemented effectively, Incident Management becomes an essential part of ITSM, ensuring that IT services are consistently reliable and that issues are resolved quickly and efficiently. By maintaining a structured approach to incident resolution, improving communication, and learning from past incidents, organizations can minimize disruptions, improve service quality, and enhance the overall user experience. Incident Management is not just about fixing problems; it is about maintaining the stability and reliability of IT services, driving continuous improvement, and ensuring that the IT department consistently meets the needs of the business and its users.

Problem Management in ITSM

Problem Management is an essential component of IT Service Management (ITSM), focused on identifying, analyzing, and addressing the root causes of incidents in IT services. While Incident Management is reactive, aiming to restore service as quickly as possible, Problem Management takes a more proactive approach, seeking to eliminate the underlying causes of recurring incidents, thereby preventing future disruptions and improving overall service reliability. The goal of Problem Management is not only to resolve individual issues but to improve the overall health of the IT environment by addressing systemic issues that could lead to further service failures.

Problem Management begins after the identification of an incident or a series of incidents that are related to the same underlying cause. Often, incidents are resolved on a case-by-case basis without fully addressing the root cause. However, when an issue recurs repeatedly or affects a significant number of users, it signals the need for a deeper investigation into the root cause. This process involves analyzing patterns and gathering data to determine why certain incidents keep happening and what needs to be done to prevent them. Through this analysis, the Problem Management team can focus their efforts on solving not just the symptoms but the underlying issues that are causing service disruptions.

The key difference between Incident Management and Problem Management is the approach. Incident Management aims to restore normal service operations as quickly as possible, minimizing the disruption to users and the business. Once the immediate issue is resolved, Incident Management typically ends. However, Problem Management focuses on long-term solutions, identifying the root cause of incidents and taking steps to prevent them from occurring in the future. This might involve analyzing system logs, reviewing historical incident data, and working with other IT teams to uncover the root cause. The goal is to eliminate the recurring problems that lead to service disruptions and improve the stability and reliability of IT services over time.

Problem Management can be broken down into two main types: reactive and proactive. Reactive Problem Management addresses problems after they have already caused incidents or disruptions, typically stemming from recurring incidents. When a pattern is identified, the Problem Management team begins its investigation into the cause. This type of Problem Management is more reactive, aiming to prevent further disruptions related to the same issue. Proactive Problem Management, on the other hand, involves identifying and addressing potential problems before they result in incidents. This could involve conducting regular reviews of system performance, analyzing incident trends, and assessing areas where the IT infrastructure may be vulnerable to failure. By adopting a proactive approach, Problem Management can help anticipate and mitigate risks, reducing the likelihood of incidents occurring in the first place.

One of the primary tasks in Problem Management is root cause analysis (RCA). RCA is a systematic process for identifying the fundamental cause of an issue. It involves digging deeper into incidents and their underlying patterns to find out why the problem happened in the first place. Root cause analysis typically involves multiple techniques, including fault tree analysis, the 5 Whys, or failure mode and effect analysis (FMEA). By identifying the root cause, Problem Management ensures that the solution addresses the issue at its source, rather than just applying a temporary fix. In many cases, the root cause may be related to faulty infrastructure, software bugs, poor configurations, or human error. Identifying these root causes is crucial for solving problems effectively and ensuring that they do not recur.

Once the root cause of a problem is identified, Problem Management moves to the resolution phase. This could involve corrective actions such as applying patches, replacing faulty hardware, reconfiguring systems, or making process improvements. Depending on the severity and complexity of the issue, the resolution might involve collaboration across various IT teams, including development, operations, and network management. In some cases, solutions may need to be tested in a controlled environment before they are deployed to production to ensure that the fix does not introduce new issues. The resolution phase is not just about addressing the problem at hand but also about ensuring that the fix is sustainable and that similar problems do not arise in the future.

Problem Management is also closely tied to Change Management. Once a problem has been identified and a solution has been proposed, the necessary changes to IT services or infrastructure must be implemented in a controlled and predictable manner. This is where Change Management comes into play, ensuring that any changes made to resolve the problem are properly tested, approved, and implemented with minimal risk to other services. Collaboration between Problem Management and Change Management is crucial to ensure that any solutions put in place are implemented in a way that does not inadvertently cause new incidents or service disruptions.

One of the benefits of effective Problem Management is that it helps reduce the volume of incidents over time. By addressing the root causes of recurring issues, organizations can reduce the frequency of incidents, leading to less disruption and a more stable IT environment. This, in turn, improves overall service quality and user satisfaction. Additionally, Problem Management can help improve the efficiency of Incident Management by reducing the number of recurring issues that IT teams need to address. As incidents are resolved more quickly and effectively, resources can be better allocated to other areas, such as proactive service improvements or innovation initiatives.

Problem Management also plays a critical role in improving the organization's overall IT strategy. By systematically identifying and addressing recurring problems, Problem Management provides valuable insights into the performance of IT services and infrastructure. This data can be used to inform future decisions about technology investments, infrastructure upgrades, and service delivery improvements. For example, if a certain hardware component or software application consistently causes problems, the Problem Management team can recommend an alternative solution or vendor that would better meet the organization's needs. By addressing systemic issues, Problem Management helps ensure that IT resources are used effectively and that the organization's IT services align with business goals.

The effectiveness of Problem Management is closely linked to the overall maturity of the IT organization. In organizations where Problem Management is well-integrated into ITSM processes, there is a greater emphasis on root cause analysis, collaboration between teams, and proactive problem resolution. In these organizations, IT teams are more likely to learn from past issues, make continuous improvements, and prevent recurring disruptions. In contrast, organizations that lack a formalized Problem Management process may continue to experience recurring incidents and inefficiencies, leading to higher costs, lower service quality, and frustrated users.

Problem Management, in the context of ITSM, provides long-term value by addressing the root causes of service disruptions and improving the reliability and stability of IT services. Through systematic root cause analysis, collaboration between teams, and proactive problem resolution, Problem Management helps organizations reduce downtime, improve service delivery, and create a more resilient IT environment. It ensures that IT teams are not just reacting to problems as they occur but are actively working to prevent future issues and enhance the overall performance of IT services. As a key component of ITSM, Problem Management ensures that IT services remain aligned with business needs, meet customer expectations, and support the ongoing success of the organization.

Configuration Management in ITSM

Configuration Management in IT Service Management (ITSM) is a critical process that focuses on systematically managing and controlling the IT assets and components within an organization's infrastructure. It ensures that all assets, from hardware and software to network devices and services, are tracked, managed, and maintained in a controlled environment. By providing a structured approach to managing IT resources, Configuration Management helps organizations maintain consistency, improve service delivery, reduce risks, and ensure that all components are aligned with business needs and objectives. The main goal of Configuration Management is to maintain an accurate and up-to-date Configuration Management Database (CMDB), which is essential for achieving effective IT service delivery, change management, incident resolution, and overall service management.

At the core of Configuration Management is the Configuration Management Database (CMDB), which acts as a centralized repository for storing information about the configuration items (CIs) within an organization's IT environment. A CI is any component or asset that needs to be managed in order to deliver an IT service. This can include servers, network devices, software applications, configurations, documentation, and even services themselves. The CMDB provides a clear and structured record of all CIs, their relationships, and dependencies. The CMDB is essential for understanding how components interact within the IT infrastructure and for managing the impact of changes or incidents on business operations. With an accurate CMDB, organizations can quickly identify the components affected by a particular change or incident and make informed decisions about how to proceed.

One of the key functions of Configuration Management is the identification and categorization of CIs. This process involves not only identifying the components within the IT infrastructure but also categorizing them based on their function, value, and importance to the business. Properly categorizing CIs allows for better management and prioritization, especially when it comes to handling incidents, changes, or service requests. For example, mission-critical servers may require a higher level of attention and a faster response time than less critical components. By categorizing CIs effectively, organizations can ensure that their IT resources are being managed in a way that aligns with business priorities and ensures that services are delivered consistently and efficiently.

Once the CIs are identified and categorized, Configuration Management also involves the process of controlling and maintaining the integrity of these components. This is particularly important when changes are made to the IT environment, such as when hardware is upgraded, software is patched, or configurations are modified. Configuration Management ensures that changes are made in a controlled and structured way, minimizing the risk of unintended consequences or disruptions to business services. By having a clear process for managing changes to CIs, organizations can ensure that all changes are tracked, approved, and properly documented. This reduces the likelihood of errors and ensures that the IT environment remains stable and secure.

Another important aspect of Configuration Management is its role in supporting change management. Changes to IT systems, whether due to software upgrades, hardware replacements, or configuration adjustments, can have significant impacts on service delivery. Configuration Management ensures that all changes are well-documented and that the relationships between CIs are understood. This is especially crucial in complex IT environments, where a change to one component can have a cascading effect on other systems and services. By maintaining an up-to-date CMDB, organizations can better assess the potential impact of changes and ensure that they are made with minimal disruption. This helps ensure that service levels are maintained and that risks associated with changes are effectively managed.

Configuration Management also supports incident management and problem management processes. When incidents occur, it is essential to understand which CIs are affected and how they relate to other components in the IT environment. The CMDB serves as a valuable tool for quickly identifying the impacted components and facilitating a faster resolution. For example, if a service disruption occurs, the service desk can use the CMDB to identify which servers, applications, or configurations are associated with the affected service. This enables them to address the issue more quickly and accurately, reducing downtime and improving the overall user experience. Similarly, in problem management, the CMDB provides valuable insights into recurring issues, helping to identify underlying causes and enabling organizations to take corrective actions to prevent future disruptions.

In addition to supporting day-to-day operations, Configuration Management plays a significant role in compliance and audit readiness. In many industries, organizations are required to adhere to strict regulatory standards regarding data security, privacy, and financial reporting. Configuration Management helps organizations maintain accurate records of their IT assets and configurations, which is essential for demonstrating compliance with these standards. The CMDB provides an auditable record of all changes made to the IT environment, including details about when changes were made, who authorized them, and what impact they had on the system. This ensures that organizations can provide the necessary documentation and evidence required for audits, reducing the risk of non-compliance and helping to avoid potential penalties.

Furthermore, Configuration Management contributes to the overall efficiency and effectiveness of IT service delivery. By maintaining an accurate and up-to-date inventory of all IT assets, organizations can optimize the use of their resources, improve decision-making, and reduce redundancy. For example, understanding the relationships between different components can help identify opportunities for consolidation or optimization, such as eliminating duplicate services or reassigning underutilized resources. The ability to quickly identify and track CIs also facilitates proactive maintenance, ensuring that systems are regularly updated, patched, and secured to prevent potential vulnerabilities.

The integration of Configuration Management with other ITSM processes is another important aspect of its effectiveness. As IT services become more interconnected, the ability to manage and monitor configurations across different systems, applications, and services is essential for maintaining service quality and stability. Configuration Management ensures that all changes, incidents, and service requests are tied back to the appropriate CIs, providing a holistic view of the IT environment. This integration helps to streamline workflows, improve communication, and enhance collaboration between IT teams. By linking Configuration Management with processes such as incident management, change management, and problem management, organizations can create a more cohesive and efficient service management framework.

One of the challenges in Configuration Management is maintaining the accuracy and completeness of the CMDB. As IT environments become more complex and dynamic, with the introduction of cloud computing, virtualization, and hybrid infrastructures, keeping the CMDB up to date can be a daunting task. Automation and discovery tools can help address this challenge by automatically detecting and recording changes to CIs in real-time. These tools can also help ensure that the CMDB remains accurate and synchronized with the live environment, reducing the risk of discrepancies and errors. However, human oversight is still required to ensure that the data captured is relevant, accurate, and meaningful.

Configuration Management also plays a key role in fostering a culture of continuous improvement within ITSM. By analyzing data from the CMDB and monitoring changes, organizations can identify areas for improvement, optimize configurations, and reduce inefficiencies. This data-driven approach enables organizations to make informed decisions about how to improve service delivery, enhance performance, and reduce costs. Configuration Management, when properly implemented and maintained, not only supports the daily operations of IT services but also provides valuable insights into the long-term health and sustainability of the IT environment.

In summary, Configuration Management in ITSM is essential for ensuring that an organization's IT infrastructure is properly tracked, managed, and maintained. It provides a structured approach to managing IT assets, supporting processes such as incident management, change management, and problem management. By maintaining an accurate CMDB and ensuring that all components are properly categorized and controlled, organizations can reduce risks, optimize resources, and improve the stability and reliability of IT services. Furthermore, Configuration Management supports compliance, audit readiness, and continual improvement, making it a vital component of an effective ITSM strategy.

Release and Deployment Management in ITSM

Release and Deployment Management is a vital process within IT Service Management (ITSM) that focuses on planning, scheduling, and controlling the movement of releases to production environments. The aim is to ensure that new or changed services are delivered smoothly, efficiently, and with minimal disruption to the business. By managing releases and deployments, organizations can ensure that new software, updates, configurations, or hardware components are introduced to their IT systems in a controlled manner, without negatively impacting service quality or business operations. This process is critical for maintaining system stability, ensuring the integrity of IT services, and enabling continuous improvement through effective and seamless transitions.

The release management process begins long before the actual deployment of new software or changes. It starts with the planning phase, where the requirements for the release are defined, including what components need to be included, the resources required, and the expected timelines. Planning also involves identifying the scope of the release, whether it is a minor patch or a major system upgrade, and ensuring that all stakeholders are aligned with the release goals. This early stage is crucial to setting expectations, ensuring that all resources and teams involved are prepared, and avoiding potential disruptions later in the process. During this phase, all necessary documentation, such as release notes and implementation guides, is also prepared, ensuring that the deployment can proceed with clear instructions for all parties involved.

One of the key objectives of Release and Deployment Management is to reduce the risk associated with introducing new services or changes. In a complex IT environment, deploying a new application or infrastructure change without proper controls can lead to service outages, security vulnerabilities, or performance issues. To mitigate these risks, the release management process includes rigorous testing phases. Before a release is deployed to production, it undergoes a series of tests in controlled environments such as development and staging. These tests may include functional testing, integration testing, load testing, and user acceptance testing, among others. This ensures that any potential issues are identified and addressed before the release is made available to end-users. Testing also validates that the new or modified service aligns with business objectives, performs as expected, and does not introduce unintended consequences to existing systems.

Once testing is complete, the deployment phase begins. Deployment involves moving the release from the development or staging environment into the live production environment. This stage requires careful coordination between various teams, including development, operations, and support staff, to ensure that the deployment process is executed efficiently and without disrupting business operations. The deployment process is typically executed during a scheduled maintenance window or during off-peak hours to minimize the impact on end-users. The deployment process can be automated to reduce human error and speed up the transition. Automation tools can streamline tasks such as code deployment, database migrations, and configuration updates, ensuring that they are executed in a consistent and repeatable manner.

In larger IT environments, especially in organizations with complex infrastructures or multiple environments, deployment may occur incrementally or in stages. For example, a release may first be deployed to a small subset of users or systems, and once it is verified to be stable and functioning as expected, it can be rolled out to the broader user base. This phased approach allows organizations to test the release in a real-world environment with a smaller group of users before committing to a full-scale deployment. It also provides an opportunity to monitor system performance and user feedback to ensure that the release is not causing unforeseen issues.

Post-deployment activities are also an integral part of the Release and Deployment Management process. After the release has been deployed to production, it is essential to monitor the service closely to ensure that it is functioning as expected. Monitoring involves checking the system's performance, tracking key metrics, and ensuring that the service is operating within agreed-upon service levels. Any issues that arise post-deployment are addressed through incident management or problem management processes. Feedback from users is collected and analyzed to identify any issues or areas for improvement. This information is used to inform future releases and ensure that the deployment process continues to improve over time.

One of the challenges of Release and Deployment Management is ensuring that it is done with minimal impact on the business and end-users. Even a well-planned release, if not properly managed, can lead to downtime, user frustration, or disruption to critical services. To mitigate these risks, it is essential to have clear communication with all stakeholders. Before a release is deployed, end-users should be informed of the upcoming changes, expected downtime, and any actions they may need to take, such as system reboots or updates. Effective communication ensures that users are prepared for the change and can minimize any potential negative impact.

Another challenge in Release and Deployment Management is managing the complexity of multiple releases. In organizations that deploy frequent updates, managing a large number of releases—each with its own timeline, dependencies, and stakeholders—can be overwhelming. This is especially true when releases are interdependent, and one release may impact the functionality of another. To manage this complexity, organizations rely on version control and release management tools to track the different versions of software, configurations, and system components. These tools provide visibility into the status of each release, its dependencies, and its relationship to other components, enabling IT teams to plan, schedule, and track releases more effectively.

Release and Deployment Management also plays a vital role in ensuring compliance with regulatory and security requirements. Many industries are subject to strict regulations that govern how software updates and changes should be managed, documented, and tested. In these environments, it is crucial that releases are carefully controlled and tracked to ensure that they meet the necessary standards. For example, in the financial services industry, organizations must ensure that all software releases are tested for security vulnerabilities and comply with data protection regulations. Release management processes ensure that all releases are properly documented, including any changes to configurations, software versions, or services, providing an audit trail for compliance purposes.

The integration of Release and Deployment Management with other ITSM processes is essential for ensuring that the deployment process aligns with broader organizational goals. Change Management, for instance, plays a significant role in ensuring that releases are assessed, approved, and planned in a structured manner. Release Management works closely with Change Management to ensure that all changes are properly reviewed, tested, and implemented with minimal risk. Similarly, Configuration Management helps ensure that all components involved in the release are properly documented and tracked. This integration between processes ensures that releases are not implemented in isolation but are part of a broader service management strategy aimed at delivering high-quality, reliable IT services.

In organizations with a high volume of releases, especially in agile or DevOps environments, automating aspects of the Release and Deployment Management process can significantly improve efficiency and reduce human error. Continuous integration and continuous delivery (CI/CD) pipelines, for example, allow organizations to automatically build, test, and deploy software updates to production environments with minimal manual intervention. This automation accelerates the release process, enabling organizations to respond more quickly to business needs and market demands.

Release and Deployment Management is a crucial process within ITSM, ensuring that new and updated services are delivered efficiently, with minimal disruption, and in alignment with business objectives. By systematically planning, testing, and deploying releases, organizations can improve service quality, enhance user experience, and maintain service continuity. Through effective management of the release process, organizations can respond to changing needs, improve system stability, and reduce the risks associated with deploying new technologies or services. Ultimately, Release and Deployment Management ensures that IT services are always evolving in line with business requirements, enabling continuous innovation and improvement.

Knowledge Management in ITSM

Knowledge Management in IT Service Management (ITSM) is a crucial process aimed at capturing, sharing, and utilizing information effectively to enhance the efficiency of IT services and improve decision-making. In a highly dynamic IT environment, where knowledge is constantly evolving, ensuring that accurate, relevant, and up-to-date information is readily available is essential for providing high-quality IT services. Knowledge Management encompasses all activities related to the creation, sharing, use, and storage of knowledge, aiming to make it accessible to the right individuals at the right time, improving both operational performance and customer satisfaction.

The importance of Knowledge Management lies in its ability to reduce inefficiencies caused by redundant processes, unproductive troubleshooting, and a lack of information. In organizations without an effective knowledge management process, employees may waste time trying to resolve issues that have already been addressed, leading to delays, frustration, and increased costs. Knowledge Management in ITSM ensures that key information is collected, organized, and easily accessible, enabling IT staff to resolve issues more efficiently and improve service delivery. The primary goal is to create a culture where knowledge is shared, and the experience and expertise within the IT organization are leveraged to improve service performance and reduce service interruptions.

A central element of Knowledge Management is the development and maintenance of a Knowledge Base, which acts as a repository for all relevant information within the organization. This Knowledge Base stores a wide range of content, from technical documentation and system configurations to troubleshooting guides, best practices, and lessons learned from previous incidents. The Knowledge Base is crucial for enabling IT teams to access accurate information quickly and efficiently, reducing the need for them to repeatedly search for solutions to common problems. By centralizing knowledge in one location, organizations can ensure that all IT staff members have access to the same information, minimizing inconsistencies and improving collaboration across teams.

In ITSM, knowledge is not limited to solving incidents or technical issues. It also includes the expertise and experience gained from handling service requests, changes, and problems. Knowledge Management ensures that the insights gained from past experiences are not lost but are systematically documented and made available for future reference. This process helps prevent recurring issues by ensuring that lessons learned from previous incidents are applied to similar situations. Knowledge sharing is critical for enabling IT staff to improve their skills and become more effective at problem-solving, enhancing the overall capability of the IT team.

Effective Knowledge Management also plays a significant role in incident resolution. When an incident occurs, one of the first steps is to identify whether it is a recurring issue. If the issue has been encountered before, the relevant knowledge can be retrieved from the Knowledge Base to expedite resolution. This not only reduces the time required to resolve incidents but also ensures that the root cause is addressed more quickly, minimizing the impact on end-users and business operations. The process of integrating Knowledge Management into Incident Management helps streamline incident resolution, enhances service reliability, and improves customer satisfaction.

Another critical aspect of Knowledge Management is the integration of this process with other ITSM processes, such as Change Management and Problem Management. In Change Management, for example, Knowledge Management helps ensure that changes to IT systems or services are documented and that the relevant information is shared with all stakeholders. This improves the planning and execution of changes, reducing the risk of errors or disruptions. In Problem Management, Knowledge Management helps IT teams to investigate and resolve recurring problems by providing them with access to historical data and solutions from similar incidents. This cross-functional collaboration ensures that knowledge is applied across various service management processes, creating a more efficient and integrated IT service environment.

A well-established Knowledge Management process also fosters a culture of continuous improvement within the IT organization. By constantly reviewing and updating the Knowledge Base with the latest insights, solutions, and best practices, organizations can ensure that their IT staff are always working with the most accurate and relevant information. This ongoing process of knowledge capture and refinement leads to better decision-making and the ability to adapt quickly to changing business requirements or technological advancements. Knowledge Management encourages employees to contribute their expertise, share solutions, and collaborate on solving complex issues, creating an environment where learning and growth are prioritized.

While knowledge sharing is essential for improving operational efficiency, it also plays a critical role in enhancing customer satisfaction. IT service teams are often the primary point of contact for end-users facing IT issues, and having access to the right knowledge allows them to resolve problems quickly and effectively. Customers expect quick and reliable solutions to their issues, and Knowledge Management enables IT teams to meet these expectations by providing them with the tools they need to deliver high-quality service. Furthermore, self-service portals that are integrated with the Knowledge Base allow users to access relevant information, solve basic issues on their own, and track the status of their service requests. This empowers users to be more self-reliant, reducing the number of service requests and improving the overall user experience.

Another important benefit of Knowledge Management is its ability to help IT organizations scale more efficiently. As organizations grow and expand, the volume of incidents, service requests, and changes typically increases, making it harder for IT teams to handle the growing demands. By ensuring that all relevant knowledge is well-documented, easily accessible, and continuously updated, Knowledge Management enables IT teams to handle an increasing workload without compromising the quality of service. This scalable approach to service delivery ensures that the IT team remains effective even as the complexity of the IT environment grows.

However, implementing Knowledge Management effectively requires overcoming several challenges. One of the main obstacles is ensuring the accuracy and relevance of the information stored in the Knowledge Base. As IT systems evolve and new technologies are introduced, older information may become obsolete or less useful. Therefore, it is critical to establish processes for regularly reviewing and updating the Knowledge Base to ensure that it remains current. Additionally, fostering a culture of knowledge sharing can be challenging, as employees may be reluctant to document their work or share their expertise. To address this, organizations must create an environment that encourages collaboration, rewards knowledge sharing, and emphasizes the importance of maintaining a high-quality Knowledge Base.

Another challenge is ensuring that knowledge is easily accessible to those who need it most. If the Knowledge Base is difficult to navigate or poorly organized, IT staff may be reluctant to use it, leading to inefficiencies in incident resolution and problem management. To address this, organizations must implement user-friendly tools that make it easy for staff to search for and retrieve relevant information quickly. The use of artificial intelligence (AI) and machine learning (ML) technologies can also help by providing smart search capabilities and automatically recommending relevant articles based on the issue at hand.

Knowledge Management is a fundamental process within ITSM that helps organizations improve service delivery, reduce incident resolution times, and foster a culture of continuous improvement. By effectively capturing, sharing, and utilizing knowledge, IT teams can deliver better outcomes, enhance customer satisfaction, and ensure that IT services are aligned with business goals. The integration of Knowledge Management into all ITSM processes ensures that the organization is always equipped with the most relevant and up-to-date information, enabling it to adapt to changes quickly, resolve issues efficiently, and drive long-term success.

Financial Management for IT Services

Financial Management for IT Services is an essential aspect of IT Service Management (ITSM) that focuses on managing the costs, budget, and financial planning of IT services and infrastructure within an organization. It ensures that IT resources are allocated effectively, that IT expenditures are controlled, and that the value of IT services is aligned with the strategic goals of the business. In an increasingly digital world, where IT is a critical enabler of business operations, financial management plays a pivotal role in maintaining a balance between providing high-quality IT services and managing costs effectively. By controlling IT spending and maximizing the value delivered by IT services, organizations can ensure that their IT investments are sustainable and contribute to long-term business success.

The primary objective of Financial Management for IT Services is to ensure that the costs of IT services are understood, tracked, and optimized throughout their lifecycle. This involves a detailed analysis of the costs associated with providing IT services, such as hardware, software, labor, and external services. Financial management ensures that IT services are delivered within budget and that any additional costs are justified and appropriately managed. It is not only about cost control, but also about ensuring that IT investments provide tangible value to the business, helping organizations optimize their IT spending while delivering services that meet business needs.

At the core of Financial Management for IT Services is the development of a comprehensive financial strategy for IT. This strategy should align with the overall business objectives of the organization and ensure that IT investments are prioritized according to their potential value. A well-defined financial strategy helps organizations allocate resources effectively, ensuring that funds are directed toward projects that will provide the greatest return on investment. This requires a deep understanding of the financial implications of IT decisions and the ability to make data-driven decisions about which projects or services to fund. It also requires ongoing financial monitoring to ensure that spending stays within the allocated budget and that any discrepancies are identified and addressed in a timely manner.

Budgeting is a key component of Financial Management for IT Services. It involves creating and managing the financial plans for IT services, ensuring that sufficient resources are allocated to support the day-to-day operations of IT services as well as planned improvements and new projects. The budgeting process should involve input from various stakeholders, including IT teams, business leaders, and financial departments, to ensure that the financial needs of both IT and the broader business are adequately met. By developing detailed budgets, organizations can ensure that they are not overspending on unnecessary resources and that funds are available to support critical IT services and initiatives. Budgeting also helps establish clear financial goals and provides a framework for measuring the success of IT investments over time.

In addition to budgeting, cost allocation is another critical aspect of financial management. Cost allocation involves assigning costs to specific IT services, projects, or departments, allowing organizations to understand where their IT spending is going and how resources are being utilized. This enables businesses to evaluate the cost-effectiveness of individual services and ensure that the most critical IT services are adequately funded. By tracking costs at a granular level, organizations can identify areas where costs can be reduced, optimize service delivery, and make informed decisions about future investments. Effective cost allocation also supports transparency and accountability, as stakeholders can see how funds are being spent and which services provide the most value to the organization.

Financial management for IT services also includes managing the financial performance of IT projects and services. It involves measuring the return on investment (ROI) for IT initiatives, ensuring that the resources invested in IT services deliver the expected benefits to the business. Financial management helps organizations assess the financial viability of IT projects, ensuring that they align with business priorities and deliver value over time. It is essential to evaluate both the direct and indirect costs of IT services and understand the total cost of ownership (TCO) for IT assets. TCO takes into account not only the initial cost of acquiring IT resources but also the ongoing costs of maintaining, supporting, and upgrading those resources throughout their lifecycle. By calculating TCO, organizations can make more informed decisions about IT investments and determine the true cost-effectiveness of their IT services.

Another important aspect of Financial Management for IT Services is the management of pricing and charging for IT services. In many organizations, IT services are provided internally to various departments or business units. In such cases, it is important to establish a pricing model that reflects the actual cost of delivering these services and ensures that the organization can recover its costs. This could involve implementing a chargeback or showback system, where business units are charged for the IT services they consume, based on usage or predefined pricing structures. These pricing models help ensure that IT services are being funded appropriately and that business units understand the financial implications of their IT consumption. Chargeback models also encourage business units to use IT resources more efficiently, as they are directly accountable for the costs incurred by their usage.

Financial management also involves risk management, as IT projects and services often come with inherent financial risks. These risks can include unexpected costs, delays, and changes in business requirements. Effective financial management ensures that potential risks are identified and mitigated early in the planning process. This might involve conducting financial risk assessments for major IT projects, developing contingency plans to address unexpected costs, and setting aside reserves to handle unforeseen expenses. By proactively managing financial risks, organizations can minimize the likelihood of cost overruns and ensure that IT services remain within budget.

Another important element of Financial Management for IT Services is the ongoing monitoring and reporting of financial performance. This involves regularly reviewing financial data, comparing actual spending to the allocated budget, and analyzing variances to determine the reasons for any discrepancies. By consistently monitoring financial performance, organizations can identify areas where costs may be creeping up or where spending can be optimized. This ongoing review process helps ensure that the financial strategy remains aligned with the organization's goals and that IT services continue to provide value without exceeding budgetary constraints. Regular reporting also ensures that stakeholders are kept informed about the financial health of IT services, fostering transparency and enabling more effective decision-making.

Effective Financial Management for IT Services also requires the involvement of cross-functional teams. Collaboration between IT, finance, and business departments is essential for aligning financial goals with organizational objectives and ensuring that IT investments support broader business strategies. Financial management in IT is not just about controlling costs; it is also about enabling the business to leverage technology to drive growth and innovation. By working together, these teams can ensure that IT investments are prioritized according to their strategic value and that financial resources are used efficiently to support business goals.

In an increasingly complex IT landscape, Financial Management for IT Services is more important than ever. It enables organizations to align IT spending with business priorities, manage costs effectively, and ensure that IT services deliver maximum value. Through budgeting, cost allocation, pricing, risk management, and performance monitoring, organizations can ensure that their IT services are financially sustainable, support business objectives, and contribute to the overall success of the organization. Financial management provides the structure and framework needed to make informed decisions about IT investments, optimize service delivery, and maintain financial control over the entire IT environment.

Capacity Management in ITSM

Capacity Management in IT Service Management (ITSM) is a crucial process that focuses on ensuring that the IT infrastructure and services have sufficient resources to meet current and future business demands. The primary objective of capacity management is to ensure that IT services are delivered at the agreed-upon performance levels while avoiding over-provisioning or under-provisioning of resources. Effective capacity management involves understanding both the current capacity of IT resources and forecasting future needs, ensuring that IT infrastructure can scale in response to business growth, technological advancements, or fluctuating demands. By balancing resource utilization and ensuring optimal performance, capacity management helps organizations deliver reliable, high-performing IT services that meet the needs of the business while controlling costs.

The process of capacity management begins with the assessment of current resources. This includes monitoring key components such as servers, storage, network bandwidth, and computing power to ensure that they are operating efficiently and that they meet the needs of the IT services they support. Data collected through performance monitoring tools and analytics is used to evaluate whether current resources are adequate to handle the volume of users, transactions, and services. Capacity management teams continually assess this data to identify any potential bottlenecks, inefficiencies, or underutilized resources. This ongoing assessment allows organizations to take proactive steps to prevent service disruptions due to resource constraints.

One of the key components of capacity management is demand management. Demand management focuses on understanding and forecasting the future demands on IT resources. It involves analyzing historical usage patterns, user behavior, business growth projections, and planned changes to IT services. By understanding the anticipated needs of the business, IT teams can better plan for capacity expansion, ensuring that resources are available when they are needed. Demand management helps to prevent both over-provisioning and under-provisioning of resources, ensuring that the right amount of capacity is available at the right time. This requires close collaboration with business units, as their needs and growth plans significantly influence IT capacity requirements.

Forecasting future capacity needs is a critical aspect of capacity management. Organizations need to predict how much IT capacity will be required to support business growth, seasonal fluctuations, or new services. Accurate forecasting helps to avoid the risks associated with capacity shortages, such as system slowdowns, outages, or poor service performance. Forecasting also helps ensure that organizations are not investing in excessive infrastructure, which can lead to unnecessary costs. Capacity management teams typically use various tools and models to analyze historical data, trends, and business forecasts to predict future demand for IT resources. These forecasts are then used to plan for upgrades, new infrastructure, or other necessary changes to meet the anticipated demands.

Capacity management is closely tied to performance management. Performance management involves monitoring the performance of IT services and ensuring that they are meeting the agreed-upon service levels, such as response times, availability, and throughput. Capacity management supports performance management by ensuring that there are sufficient resources available to meet these performance targets. If resources are stretched too thin or if there is insufficient capacity, performance issues such as slow response times, system downtime, or degradation in service quality may occur. Capacity management helps prevent such issues by continuously monitoring resource utilization and ensuring that resources are scaled appropriately to meet performance requirements. This alignment between capacity and performance ensures that IT services consistently meet business expectations and user demands.

Another important aspect of capacity management is the management of infrastructure lifecycle. As IT infrastructure evolves and becomes more complex, it is essential to manage the entire lifecycle of hardware, software, and network resources. This includes ensuring that aging equipment is replaced, outdated systems are retired, and new systems are introduced as needed to support business requirements. Capacity management teams must ensure that infrastructure upgrades are planned in advance and that new technologies are integrated seamlessly into the existing environment. This proactive approach helps organizations maintain system reliability, reduce downtime, and optimize performance throughout the lifecycle of their IT infrastructure.

When implementing capacity management, organizations must also consider scalability. Scalability refers to the ability of an IT system to handle increasing workloads by adding resources or expanding infrastructure without compromising performance. Scalability is particularly important in dynamic business environments where demand for IT services can fluctuate rapidly. Capacity management ensures that IT systems are designed to scale effectively, whether through cloud computing, virtualization, or other technologies that enable the addition of resources without major disruptions. By planning for scalability, organizations can ensure that their IT infrastructure can grow in line with business needs, supporting new services, users, or locations as required.

In addition to technical considerations, capacity management also involves managing costs. One of the challenges of capacity management is balancing the need for sufficient capacity with the need to control costs. Over-provisioning resources can lead to unnecessary costs, while under-provisioning can lead to performance degradation or service disruptions. Capacity management teams must work closely with financial and business teams to ensure that investments in infrastructure are justified and aligned with the organization's budget and strategic goals. By carefully managing capacity, organizations can optimize the use of their IT resources, minimize waste, and ensure that investments in infrastructure deliver the maximum value.

Effective capacity management also requires ongoing communication and collaboration between IT teams, business units, and other stakeholders. IT departments must understand the business's goals, growth plans, and changing needs to forecast and plan for future capacity requirements accurately. Business units, on the other hand, must communicate their upcoming needs, such as the introduction of new services or anticipated increases in users or transactions, to ensure that IT resources are available to support them. This collaborative approach ensures that capacity management is aligned with the business strategy and that resources are allocated effectively to meet both current and future demands.

Capacity management must also be flexible enough to respond to unexpected changes in demand. While forecasting is an essential part of capacity planning, unforeseen events such as system failures, sudden increases in user activity, or unexpected business growth can strain capacity. In these cases, capacity management teams must be able to quickly assess the situation, identify the resources that are under strain, and make adjustments to ensure that services remain available. This may involve temporarily increasing resource availability, reallocating resources, or deploying additional infrastructure to meet the immediate demand. Flexibility and responsiveness are key to ensuring that IT services can handle unpredictable spikes in demand without compromising performance.

An essential tool for capacity management is the use of monitoring and reporting systems. These systems provide real-time visibility into resource utilization and performance, enabling capacity management teams to identify issues before they impact service delivery. By continuously monitoring resource usage, IT teams can track trends, identify inefficiencies, and take corrective actions as needed. Monitoring tools also provide valuable data that can be used for forecasting future capacity requirements and for optimizing resource allocation. These tools play a crucial role in maintaining system performance and ensuring that resources are being used effectively.

In summary, Capacity Management in ITSM is essential for ensuring that IT resources are sufficient to meet current and future business needs while maintaining performance and controlling costs. By continually monitoring resource usage, forecasting future demand, managing infrastructure lifecycle, and collaborating with business units, capacity management enables organizations to deliver reliable IT services that support business growth and efficiency. With effective capacity management, IT teams can optimize their resources, improve service quality, and ensure that the IT infrastructure remains scalable and responsive to changing business requirements.

Availability Management in ITSM

Availability Management in IT Service Management (ITSM) is a critical process designed to ensure that IT services and systems are consistently available to meet the needs of the business and its users. Availability refers to the ability of an IT service or component to perform its required functions when needed. The goal of Availability Management is to ensure that the right levels of availability are provided to users, minimizing downtime and disruptions while supporting business continuity. This process involves designing, managing, and optimizing IT services and systems to ensure that they meet the agreed-upon availability requirements, which are typically defined in service level agreements (SLAs).

One of the core components of Availability Management is the development and management of service availability objectives. These objectives are typically based on business needs and are reflected in the SLAs between IT and the business. Availability Management works closely with business units to understand their needs and define what level of availability is required for different services. For example, critical business applications may need to be available 24/7, while other non-essential services may only require uptime during business hours. By understanding the specific needs of the business, IT teams can tailor availability strategies to ensure that services are provided at the appropriate level of performance and reliability.

Availability Management also involves ensuring that IT systems and services are resilient and capable of recovering quickly from disruptions. One key aspect of resilience is redundancy, which involves having backup systems, processes, or resources in place to ensure continuity in case of failure. This can include backup servers, alternate network routes, or replicated databases. By designing IT systems with redundancy in mind, organizations can ensure that critical services remain available even in the event of a failure. In addition to redundancy, availability management focuses on fault tolerance, ensuring that systems can continue to operate even if certain components fail. This is particularly important in environments where high availability is essential, such as financial services or healthcare, where downtime can result in significant consequences.

Capacity planning is closely linked to availability management. It is essential to ensure that systems are not only resilient but also appropriately scaled to meet current and future demand. Inadequate capacity can lead to performance degradation or service unavailability during periods of high demand. Availability Management involves regularly assessing the capacity of systems and ensuring that there is enough resource headroom to handle peak usage without compromising service quality. This includes monitoring key metrics such as server utilization, network bandwidth, and storage capacity to identify potential bottlenecks or areas where additional resources may be needed. By aligning capacity planning with availability goals, organizations can ensure that they are prepared to meet changing demands while maintaining high levels of service availability.

Another important aspect of Availability Management is proactive monitoring and maintenance. IT systems and services must be continually monitored to detect issues before they result in service disruptions. This involves using monitoring tools to track system performance, availability, and key health indicators in real-time. Proactive monitoring allows IT teams to identify potential issues early, such as performance degradation, hardware failures, or network congestion, and take corrective action before they lead to a service outage. Monitoring tools can also generate alerts that notify IT staff when availability thresholds are at risk, enabling them to respond quickly and prevent issues from escalating into major disruptions.

In addition to monitoring, regular maintenance is essential to ensure the ongoing availability of IT services. This includes routine activities such as applying software patches, upgrading hardware, and performing system health checks. Scheduled maintenance is often planned during off-peak hours to minimize the impact on users, but it is critical to ensure that any maintenance activities are well-coordinated to prevent unplanned downtime. By maintaining systems and infrastructure proactively, Availability Management helps prevent failures caused by outdated software, unsupported hardware, or other preventable issues. This proactive approach to maintenance helps ensure that services remain stable, secure, and available for users.

Incident Management is another key process that closely interacts with Availability Management. When an incident occurs, the availability of the affected service is compromised, and the primary goal of Incident Management is to restore service as quickly as possible. Availability Management teams work closely with Incident Management to ensure that there are clear processes in place for addressing service disruptions and minimizing downtime. After the incident is resolved, Availability Management teams conduct post-incident reviews to analyze the cause of the disruption and ensure that corrective actions are taken to prevent similar issues in the future. This continuous feedback loop between Availability and Incident Management helps improve overall service availability over time.

Problem Management is also an important aspect of maintaining high availability. When recurring incidents or service disruptions are identified, they may indicate underlying problems that need to be addressed to improve service availability. Problem Management focuses on identifying the root causes of recurring issues and implementing long-term solutions to eliminate them. Availability Management works with Problem Management to ensure that systemic issues are addressed and that the necessary improvements are made to prevent further disruptions. This collaboration helps ensure that availability goals are met and that services are resilient to both expected and unexpected challenges.

An essential part of Availability Management is understanding and managing the availability of third-party services. Many organizations rely on external vendors or cloud service providers to deliver critical IT services, and any downtime or service disruptions from these third parties can impact overall service availability. Availability Management must work with these vendors to ensure that their services meet the agreed-upon availability levels, often defined in Service Level Agreements (SLAs) or contracts. This includes monitoring third-party services, evaluating their performance, and ensuring that any disruptions are addressed quickly and effectively. In cases where third-party availability is critical, Availability Management may require contingency plans, such as backup providers or alternative services, to mitigate risks and ensure continued service delivery.

Availability Management also plays a crucial role in disaster recovery and business continuity planning. In the event of a major disruption, such as a natural disaster, cyberattack, or data center failure, organizations must be able to quickly recover their IT services to maintain business operations. Availability Management ensures that robust disaster recovery plans are in place, which may include data backups, failover systems, and procedures for restoring services. By incorporating availability and recovery strategies into disaster recovery planning, organizations can ensure that they are prepared for unforeseen events and that critical services can be restored as quickly as possible with minimal data loss.

Effective communication is another key component of Availability Management. Throughout the process of maintaining and improving service availability, it is essential that stakeholders, including business leaders, IT teams, and end-users, are kept informed of availability-related issues. This includes providing regular reports on system performance, availability, and any disruptions that have occurred, as well as communicating planned maintenance schedules and potential risks to availability. Clear communication helps manage expectations and ensures that users are aware of any potential impact to services.

Availability Management in ITSM is essential for ensuring that IT services meet the availability requirements of the business. By proactively managing service availability through monitoring, maintenance, and capacity planning, organizations can ensure that their IT systems are reliable, resilient, and scalable. Availability Management also helps organizations recover quickly from disruptions and minimize the impact on users and business operations. By working closely with other ITSM processes, such as Incident Management, Problem Management, and Change Management, Availability Management contributes to the overall effectiveness of IT service delivery, helping organizations provide high-quality, dependable services that meet the needs of the business.

Security Management in ITSM

Security Management in IT Service Management (ITSM) is a vital process that focuses on protecting the confidentiality, integrity, and availability of IT services and systems. As organizations become more reliant on technology, the need for robust security practices to protect sensitive data and ensure operational continuity has become more critical than ever. Security management within ITSM aims to safeguard IT services against a wide range of potential threats, including cyberattacks, data breaches, system failures, and internal misconfigurations. By integrating security considerations into all aspects of IT service delivery, organizations can proactively manage risks, protect business assets, and ensure compliance with regulatory requirements.

The core principle of Security Management is to ensure that appropriate security measures are in place to mitigate risks while enabling the organization to achieve its business goals. This involves identifying and assessing potential security threats and vulnerabilities, implementing preventative measures, and continuously monitoring and responding to security incidents. One of the primary goals of security management is to establish a security framework that aligns with the organization's broader business strategy, ensuring that security efforts support organizational objectives rather than hinder them. The process involves collaboration across various teams, including IT operations, business units, and third-party vendors, to create a cohesive and comprehensive security strategy.

Risk management is a key element of Security Management within ITSM. Organizations must continuously assess the risks associated with their IT systems, applications, and data. This includes identifying potential threats, such as hacking attempts, data leaks, insider threats, or hardware failures, and evaluating their potential impact on the organization. Once the risks have been identified, security management teams work to implement controls and strategies that minimize the likelihood and impact of these threats. Risk assessments are typically conducted regularly and are updated based on changes in the IT environment, emerging threats, or new business requirements. By identifying and mitigating risks, security management helps prevent security incidents before they occur and ensures that the organization is prepared to respond to any unforeseen events.

A key component of Security Management is the management of access control and user authentication. Protecting sensitive data and IT services begins with ensuring that only authorized users have access to critical systems and information. This is achieved through the implementation of access control policies, which define who can access specific resources, what actions they are allowed to perform, and under what conditions. User authentication processes, such as multi-factor authentication (MFA), help ensure that users are properly verified before being granted access to IT systems. By implementing strict access control and authentication measures, organizations can significantly reduce the risk of unauthorized access and data breaches.

Data protection is another essential aspect of Security Management in ITSM. With the increasing volume of sensitive information stored and transmitted across IT systems, organizations must ensure that this data is adequately protected from loss, theft, or corruption. This includes implementing encryption methods to protect data in transit and at rest, as well as ensuring that data is securely backed up to prevent loss in the event of a system failure or cyberattack. Data protection also extends to ensuring that personal data is handled in compliance with regulatory frameworks, such as the General Data Protection Regulation (GDPR) in Europe. By focusing on data protection, security management ensures that the organization can maintain user trust, meet legal requirements, and prevent data breaches that could result in significant financial and reputational damage.

Incident Management plays a critical role in Security Management. Despite best efforts to prevent security threats, incidents such as cyberattacks or data breaches can still occur. Security incident management involves identifying, analyzing, and responding to security breaches in a structured and efficient manner. When a security incident occurs, the priority is to contain the threat, limit the damage, and restore normal service as quickly as possible. Security incident management teams work closely with other ITSM processes, such as Incident Management, to ensure that security incidents are handled promptly and effectively. Once the incident is contained, a post-incident review is conducted to determine the root cause of the breach and identify any weaknesses in the security framework. This continuous feedback loop helps organizations strengthen their security posture and prevent future incidents.

Compliance management is another crucial aspect of Security Management. Organizations are often subject to a wide range of legal and regulatory requirements related to data security, privacy, and IT governance. Compliance with these regulations is essential to avoid legal penalties, protect customer trust, and ensure that IT services are delivered securely. Security management teams are responsible for ensuring that the organization's security practices align with applicable regulations, such as HIPAA, PCI-DSS, or SOX, and that appropriate documentation is in place to demonstrate compliance during audits. By maintaining a robust compliance framework, organizations can avoid the risks associated with non-compliance, including financial penalties and reputational damage.

Another key responsibility of Security Management is ensuring the security of third-party services and vendors. In many modern IT environments, organizations rely on third-party providers for cloud services, software solutions, and other outsourced IT functions. These external providers must meet the organization's security standards to ensure that data and systems are protected. Security management teams work with third-party vendors to establish security requirements, monitor their compliance, and ensure that adequate security measures are in place. This includes conducting regular security assessments, reviewing vendor security practices, and ensuring that third-party contracts include appropriate security clauses. By managing third-party security risks, organizations can mitigate the potential vulnerabilities introduced by external providers and ensure that their IT ecosystem remains secure.

Security Management in ITSM also emphasizes the importance of training and awareness. While technological tools and systems are essential for maintaining security, human factors often play a critical role in preventing security breaches. Employees must be trained to recognize and respond to security threats, such as phishing attacks, password security, and secure handling of sensitive information. Security awareness programs help ensure that all staff members understand their role in maintaining the security of IT services and are equipped with the knowledge and skills necessary to identify and address potential threats. By fostering a culture of security awareness, organizations can reduce the risk of human error and strengthen their overall security posture.

A proactive approach to security is fundamental to effective Security Management. Rather than only reacting to incidents or breaches, security management teams work to anticipate and prevent potential threats. This includes conducting regular vulnerability assessments, penetration testing, and security audits to identify weaknesses in the IT environment. Security management teams also stay informed about emerging threats, such as new malware or hacking techniques, and update security measures accordingly. By maintaining a proactive security strategy, organizations can stay ahead of evolving threats and ensure that their IT services remain secure and resilient.

In summary, Security Management in ITSM plays a crucial role in protecting the organization's IT services, systems, and data from a wide range of potential security threats. Through risk management, access control, data protection, incident management, compliance, and vendor management, Security Management ensures that IT services are delivered securely and in alignment with business goals. By integrating security practices across all IT service processes, organizations can mitigate risks, improve operational resilience, and build trust with customers and stakeholders. The proactive, continuous nature of Security Management ensures that security remains a top priority and that the organization is prepared to respond to threats effectively, protecting both its assets and its reputation.

ITSM Metrics and KPIs

In IT Service Management (ITSM), the use of metrics and Key Performance Indicators (KPIs) is essential for assessing the effectiveness, efficiency, and overall quality of IT services. Metrics provide quantifiable data that reflects the performance of IT services, while KPIs are the specific, measurable values used to track progress toward achieving defined business objectives. These tools are crucial for organizations seeking to align their IT services with business needs, improve service delivery, and ensure that IT operations contribute positively to the overall goals of the organization. By measuring and evaluating performance, ITSM teams can identify areas of improvement, streamline processes, and ensure that IT services meet the expectations of both users and business stakeholders.

One of the primary purposes of ITSM metrics and KPIs is to enable organizations to track and measure the success of their IT services. This includes monitoring how well IT services are being delivered, whether service levels are being met, and how efficiently resources are being utilized. Metrics and KPIs are used to evaluate key service management processes, such as incident management, change management, problem management, and service request fulfillment. These metrics provide insight into how well ITSM processes are functioning, highlight areas where performance may be lacking, and guide efforts to optimize service delivery.

In Incident Management, for example, common metrics include incident resolution time, first-contact resolution rate, and the number of incidents reopened. These metrics help IT teams measure how quickly incidents are being resolved, how effectively they are being handled on the first contact, and whether incidents are being appropriately closed or require further attention. KPIs in this context might include targets such as resolving 80% of incidents within a certain timeframe or ensuring that 90% of incidents are resolved during the first contact. By tracking these metrics and KPIs, ITSM teams can monitor their performance and make data-driven decisions to improve incident management processes.

Another key area of ITSM where metrics and KPIs are crucial is in Change Management. Effective change management ensures that changes to IT systems are implemented with minimal disruption and that they meet business needs. Metrics in this area might include the number of changes implemented successfully, the percentage of changes made on time, or the percentage of changes that result in incidents or problems. KPIs could include targets such as achieving a 95% success rate for all changes or ensuring that 90% of changes are completed within the planned window. These metrics and KPIs help ITSM teams measure how well changes are being managed and whether any changes are causing disruptions to the services or systems.

Problem Management also relies heavily on metrics to evaluate its success. Problem management aims to identify and eliminate the root causes of recurring incidents, thus reducing service disruptions over time. Metrics for problem management may include the number of problems identified, the time taken to resolve problems, and the reduction in recurring incidents after problem resolution. KPIs in problem management could include the goal of reducing recurring incidents by a certain percentage over a given period. By measuring these metrics and tracking performance, ITSM teams can identify whether their problem management processes are effective in preventing future incidents and improving service reliability.

Service Request Management is another area where KPIs and metrics are essential. This process ensures that service requests from users are handled efficiently and in accordance with predefined service level agreements (SLAs). Metrics in this area might include the number of service requests fulfilled within the agreed time frame, the percentage of service requests resolved within SLA, and the number of requests handled by automated systems or self-service portals. KPIs could include achieving a target fulfillment rate for service requests, such as 95% of requests being completed within a certain number of hours. Monitoring these metrics helps ITSM teams ensure that service requests are processed efficiently, helping users get the services they need quickly and reducing the overall workload on IT staff.

While metrics and KPIs provide valuable data on the performance of ITSM processes, they also serve a broader purpose in helping organizations achieve their strategic business goals. By aligning IT services with business priorities, ITSM teams can use metrics to evaluate how well their services support business objectives. For instance, if a company is focused on improving customer satisfaction, KPIs related to service availability, incident resolution times, and user satisfaction ratings become critical in measuring the success of IT services in meeting this goal. By continuously measuring and analyzing performance against these KPIs, ITSM teams can demonstrate the value of IT services to the business and make informed decisions about where to invest resources for improvement.

To ensure that ITSM metrics and KPIs are effective, it is important that they are aligned with the organization's overall objectives and that they are realistic, measurable, and actionable. Setting appropriate KPIs requires a deep understanding of both the IT service delivery process and the business needs. ITSM teams must work closely with business stakeholders to ensure that the metrics they track are aligned with the goals of the organization. For example, if the organization is focused on reducing downtime, KPIs related to system availability, incident response times, and mean time to recovery (MTTR) would be crucial. Clear and well-defined KPIs allow IT teams to focus on the most important areas, allocate resources effectively, and drive improvements that support the business strategy.

In addition to measuring performance, ITSM metrics and KPIs are essential for continuous improvement. By tracking and analyzing these metrics over time, organizations can identify trends, recognize patterns, and spot areas where improvements can be made. For example, if a particular service is consistently falling short of its availability target, IT teams can investigate the root cause and implement corrective actions to improve service delivery. Metrics and KPIs also enable ITSM teams to assess the impact of changes or process improvements, helping to determine whether the adjustments have had the desired effect on service performance.

It is also important for organizations to regularly review and adjust their KPIs to ensure that they remain relevant and aligned with evolving business priorities. As business needs change, so too should the metrics and KPIs that are used to measure IT service performance. Periodically reassessing KPIs helps organizations adapt to new challenges, technologies, and objectives, ensuring that ITSM processes remain aligned with the organization's evolving strategic goals. This flexibility ensures that metrics continue to provide valuable insights and drive improvements that contribute to the success of the business.

A key aspect of effectively utilizing ITSM metrics and KPIs is the communication of results to relevant stakeholders. Sharing performance data with leadership and other business units helps demonstrate the value of IT services and the contribution of IT to the overall business objectives. It also facilitates informed decision-making, as stakeholders can use the data to prioritize investments, allocate resources, and make adjustments to IT strategies. Transparent reporting of metrics and KPIs fosters a culture of accountability and continuous improvement, where IT teams and business units work together to achieve common goals.

In summary, ITSM metrics and KPIs are essential for measuring the performance, effectiveness, and value of IT services. By tracking key processes such as incident management, change management, problem management, and service request fulfillment, organizations can ensure that their IT services are aligned with business needs and objectives. These metrics provide valuable insights into performance, enabling IT teams to identify areas for improvement, optimize service delivery, and demonstrate the value of IT services to the organization. Through continuous measurement, analysis, and improvement, ITSM metrics and KPIs help organizations maintain high-quality, efficient IT services that support business success.

Integrating ITSM with Business Processes

The integration of IT Service Management (ITSM) with business processes is a vital aspect of ensuring that IT services align with the strategic goals and needs of the organization. In today's increasingly technology-driven world, IT is not only a support function but also a crucial enabler of business operations. IT services must be seamlessly integrated with business processes to ensure that both the technology infrastructure and the business can work in tandem to achieve common objectives. This integration is essential for improving efficiency, enhancing service delivery, and ultimately driving business success.

ITSM frameworks like ITIL (Information Technology Infrastructure Library) are designed to ensure that IT services meet the needs of the business. By integrating ITSM with business processes, organizations can create a more cohesive IT environment that supports business goals while maintaining high-quality service delivery. This alignment allows IT teams to better understand business requirements, provide the necessary resources, and ensure that technology supports the operational and strategic objectives of the organization.

One of the key benefits of integrating ITSM with business processes is the ability to improve service delivery. When IT services are closely aligned with business processes, IT teams can tailor their services to meet the specific needs of different business units. For example, IT services that support customer-facing functions, such as customer service or e-commerce platforms, may have different performance requirements than those supporting internal business operations, such as accounting or HR. By understanding the distinct needs of each business process, IT teams can design and deliver IT services that are optimized for performance, reliability, and scalability, ensuring that they directly support the organization's operational goals.

Moreover, this integration allows for more efficient resource allocation. IT resources, such as hardware, software, and personnel, are often costly and limited. By aligning IT service delivery with business priorities, organizations can ensure that their IT resources are directed toward projects that provide the most value. For instance, by understanding which business processes are critical to achieving strategic goals, IT teams can prioritize the allocation of resources to those services, ensuring that the organization's most important business functions are adequately supported. This strategic allocation helps optimize both IT and business operations, leading to cost savings and more effective use of resources.

Another significant advantage of integrating ITSM with business processes is the enhancement of agility. In today's fast-paced business environment, organizations need to respond quickly to changing market conditions, customer demands, and new business opportunities. IT services must be adaptable and able to scale rapidly to meet these dynamic needs. By aligning ITSM practices with business processes, organizations can create a more agile IT environment that can quickly adapt to new business requirements. For example, if a business unit needs to launch a new product or service, IT teams can ensure that the necessary infrastructure and support services are in place to meet this demand quickly and efficiently. This agility is critical for staying competitive and ensuring that IT services remain aligned with evolving business priorities.

Furthermore, the integration of ITSM with business processes improves communication and collaboration between IT and business teams. Traditionally, IT has often been seen as a separate department that supports the business but operates independently. However, in organizations where IT is integrated with business processes, IT teams become more closely involved in business strategy and decision-making. This collaboration fosters a better understanding of business needs and helps IT teams design services that support those needs effectively. Regular communication between IT and business teams ensures that both sides are aligned on objectives, performance expectations, and the necessary resources, which leads to smoother operations and improved service delivery.

The integration of ITSM with business processes also facilitates better governance and compliance. As organizations increasingly rely on technology to drive their operations, they must ensure that their IT services comply with internal policies, industry standards, and regulatory requirements. Integrating ITSM with business processes helps create a unified framework for managing compliance, ensuring that IT services adhere to the necessary standards while supporting business operations. For example, when deploying IT services that handle sensitive data, such as customer information or financial records, ITSM processes can ensure that these services meet privacy and security requirements, reducing the risk of non-compliance. This integration helps mitigate risks, maintain operational integrity, and ensure that the organization remains in compliance with legal and regulatory requirements.

Additionally, integrating ITSM with business processes improves the overall customer experience. IT services play a crucial role in delivering seamless and efficient customer interactions, whether through customer support, e-commerce platforms, or internal applications used by customer service teams. By aligning IT service management with the needs of the customer-facing business processes, organizations can ensure that their IT services are designed to meet customer expectations and provide a positive experience. For example, if an e-commerce platform experiences downtime, it directly impacts customer satisfaction and sales. By integrating ITSM practices, such as incident management and service continuity planning, with the platform's business processes, IT teams can ensure rapid recovery and minimize disruptions to the customer experience.

Moreover, integrating ITSM with business processes supports the continual improvement of both IT and business operations. ITSM frameworks emphasize the importance of continual service improvement (CSI), which involves regularly reviewing and optimizing IT services based on performance data, feedback, and business requirements. When ITSM is integrated with business processes, this continual improvement extends beyond IT services and encompasses the entire business operation. For example, performance data from IT systems can provide valuable insights into the efficiency of business processes, enabling both IT and business teams to identify areas for improvement. This iterative approach to improvement fosters a culture of innovation, helping organizations adapt to changing market conditions and business needs.

To achieve successful integration, organizations need to adopt a holistic approach that involves both IT and business stakeholders. This means that IT teams must have a deep understanding of business processes, and business teams must recognize the importance of technology in achieving their objectives. Cross-functional collaboration, shared goals, and mutual understanding are essential to ensure that both IT and business teams are working toward the same objectives. Regular feedback loops between IT and business teams allow both sides to evaluate progress, discuss challenges, and make adjustments as needed. This collaborative approach ensures that IT services are continuously aligned with business needs and that both IT and business teams are working together to achieve organizational goals.

In addition, organizations must ensure that they have the right tools, technologies, and frameworks in place to support the integration of ITSM with business processes. This may involve adopting ITSM platforms that provide a unified view of IT services, performance metrics, and business processes, allowing IT and business teams to collaborate effectively. These platforms can also support automation, streamlining workflows, and improving efficiency across both IT and business operations.

In summary, integrating ITSM with business processes is essential for ensuring that IT services are aligned with the needs of the business. This integration improves service delivery, enhances agility, optimizes resource allocation, fosters collaboration, and ensures compliance with regulatory standards. By working together, IT and business teams can deliver IT services that drive business success, enhance the customer experience, and support the organization's strategic objectives. With the right tools, processes, and collaboration, organizations can create a cohesive IT environment that supports their business goals and ensures long-term success.

ITSM for Cloud Services

The integration of IT Service Management (ITSM) with cloud services is an evolving area of focus for organizations seeking to optimize their use of cloud technology while maintaining high standards of service delivery. As businesses increasingly migrate to the cloud, the need to apply ITSM best practices to cloud services becomes more apparent. Cloud services offer scalability, flexibility, and cost savings, but they also introduce new challenges in terms of service management, security, and integration with existing IT infrastructures. The adoption of ITSM frameworks like ITIL in cloud environments helps organizations ensure that cloud services are managed efficiently and effectively, aligning them with business needs and ensuring that they meet the required performance and availability levels.

Cloud services, unlike traditional on-premise IT systems, offer resources that are highly dynamic and scalable, with users being able to rapidly provision and decommission services. This flexibility introduces a level of complexity to service management that requires organizations to rethink how they apply ITSM processes such as incident management, problem management, and change management. The need to manage cloud resources efficiently, while ensuring that they meet service level agreements (SLAs) and provide the expected value to the business, is a key driver for integrating ITSM into cloud services.

A critical aspect of applying ITSM to cloud services is the alignment of cloud-based service delivery with business objectives. As with traditional IT services, organizations must ensure that cloud services meet agreed-upon availability, performance, and security standards.

One of the main challenges in cloud service management is that many organizations rely on third-party cloud service providers, making it more difficult to directly manage and monitor the performance of cloud resources. ITSM frameworks help address this challenge by establishing clear processes for managing cloud services, setting expectations with providers, and ensuring that cloud services are delivered in line with business priorities.

Service level management plays a key role in ensuring that cloud services meet the needs of the business. In a traditional IT environment, service level agreements (SLAs) are typically negotiated between the IT department and internal business units. With cloud services, however, SLAs are often negotiated between the organization and the cloud service provider. These agreements define the performance, availability, and support levels that the provider is obligated to meet. ITSM frameworks help organizations define, monitor, and enforce these SLAs, ensuring that cloud services are delivered in accordance with business requirements. Regular reviews of service performance are conducted to ensure that cloud services continue to meet the agreed-upon standards, and any breaches or issues are addressed promptly.

Another essential ITSM process that applies to cloud services is incident management. In cloud environments, incidents can arise from a variety of factors, including service outages, performance degradation, or integration issues between cloud and on-premise systems. ITSM best practices guide organizations in responding to incidents promptly, ensuring that cloud services are restored as quickly as possible to minimize disruption. In many cases, incidents related to cloud services require collaboration between internal IT teams and the cloud service provider to identify the cause and implement a resolution. Incident management processes within ITSM ensure that these incidents are tracked, managed, and resolved according to predefined processes, helping to reduce downtime and improve overall service reliability.

Problem management is another critical area of ITSM that must be applied to cloud services. In cloud environments, the root cause of recurring incidents may not always be immediately apparent, especially if the organization relies on external cloud service providers.

Problem management helps organizations identify and resolve underlying issues that cause repeated incidents, whether they are related to infrastructure, software configurations, or service dependencies. ITSM provides a structured framework for investigating recurring issues, collaborating with cloud providers, and implementing long-term solutions to prevent future incidents. By focusing on problem resolution, organizations can enhance the stability of their cloud services and reduce the likelihood of service disruptions.

Change management is particularly important when managing cloud services. Cloud environments are highly dynamic, with the need to frequently update software, deploy new services, and scale resources up or down in response to business needs. In traditional IT environments, change management processes ensure that changes are implemented in a controlled manner, minimizing disruptions to service delivery. Cloud services introduce new complexities in this area, as organizations must coordinate changes with their cloud service providers while ensuring that the changes do not affect service availability or performance. ITSM best practices for change management help organizations plan, schedule, and implement changes to cloud services in a structured way, ensuring that these changes align with business requirements and are executed with minimal risk.

Capacity management is an area where cloud services provide both challenges and opportunities. Cloud computing offers scalability, allowing organizations to rapidly adjust resources to meet demand. However, this flexibility also means that capacity management processes must be adapted to ensure that cloud resources are appropriately provisioned and optimized. ITSM frameworks help organizations track resource utilization in the cloud, forecast future demand, and ensure that cloud services are scaled appropriately to meet business needs. This involves monitoring key performance indicators such as resource utilization, response times, and service availability, and using this data to make informed decisions about resource allocation and scaling.

Security management is another key consideration when integrating ITSM with cloud services. Security in the cloud is a shared responsibility between the organization and the cloud service provider.

While the provider is responsible for securing the infrastructure, the organization must ensure that its data and applications are protected. ITSM frameworks support organizations in managing security risks by defining security policies, monitoring compliance, and ensuring that appropriate security controls are in place for cloud services. This includes data encryption, access control, incident response planning, and monitoring for potential threats. By incorporating security management processes into ITSM practices, organizations can ensure that their cloud services are secure, comply with regulatory requirements, and minimize the risk of data breaches or other security incidents.

An additional challenge in managing cloud services within ITSM is the integration of cloud services with on-premise IT systems. Many organizations operate hybrid environments, where cloud resources are integrated with traditional, on-premise IT systems. This creates the need for seamless integration between cloud services and internal IT infrastructure to ensure that business processes can operate smoothly across both environments. ITSM frameworks help organizations manage these integrations, ensuring that both cloud and on-premise services are properly aligned and functioning together to support the organization's goals.

Furthermore, organizations must adopt an effective monitoring and reporting strategy for cloud services. ITSM frameworks emphasize the importance of performance monitoring, and this is particularly relevant in cloud environments, where service delivery can vary based on a number of factors. Monitoring tools within ITSM frameworks provide real-time visibility into the performance and availability of cloud services, enabling organizations to detect issues quickly and take corrective action before they impact users. Reporting also allows organizations to track cloud service performance against SLAs, ensuring that the cloud services provided meet the expected standards and any breaches are identified and addressed promptly.

Integrating ITSM with cloud services requires a holistic approach that aligns cloud service management with broader business and IT goals. By applying ITSM principles such as incident management, change management, problem management, and capacity management to cloud services, organizations can ensure that they are effectively managing their cloud resources and delivering high-quality services to meet business needs. This integration helps organizations balance the flexibility and scalability of cloud services with the need for structured, reliable service delivery, allowing them to fully leverage the benefits of cloud computing while maintaining control over service quality, performance, and security.

ITSM in a Digital Transformation Era

The concept of IT Service Management (ITSM) has evolved significantly over the years, especially in the context of the digital transformation era. Digital transformation refers to the integration of digital technology into all areas of a business, fundamentally changing how the organization operates and delivers value to its customers. This shift has brought about profound changes in the way IT services are managed, requiring organizations to adapt their ITSM practices to meet the demands of a rapidly changing technological landscape. As businesses increasingly rely on cloud computing, artificial intelligence, automation, and other digital tools, ITSM must evolve to support these innovations and help organizations achieve their transformation goals.

At its core, ITSM is about delivering high-quality IT services that meet the needs of the business. However, in the digital transformation era, ITSM practices must go beyond traditional service delivery to accommodate the complex and dynamic nature of modern technology environments. The integration of emerging technologies and the growing expectation for faster, more agile service delivery have shifted the focus of ITSM from managing traditional on-premise IT systems to overseeing cloud services, mobile platforms, and decentralized networks. This shift requires a rethinking of how services are delivered, how performance is measured, and how IT teams interact with the broader organization.

One of the most significant impacts of digital transformation on ITSM is the increased need for agility and speed. In the past, ITSM processes like change management, incident management, and service request fulfillment were often seen as rigid, with lengthy approval processes and fixed timelines. However, in the digital age, businesses need to move faster to remain competitive. ITSM frameworks must be more flexible and responsive to accommodate the speed of business changes. Agile methodologies and DevOps practices have become integral to ITSM as they emphasize quick iterations, continuous improvement, and seamless collaboration between IT and business teams. By adopting these methodologies, organizations can align their ITSM practices with the fast-paced nature of digital transformation, enabling them to deploy new services, updates, and features more quickly and efficiently.

Automation is another key factor driving the evolution of ITSM in the digital transformation era. As businesses scale and adopt new technologies, the complexity of managing IT services increases. To keep up with these changes, organizations are turning to automation to streamline ITSM processes. Automating routine tasks such as incident logging, ticket assignment, and service request fulfillment helps reduce the administrative burden on IT teams, allowing them to focus on more strategic initiatives. Automation also enhances the consistency and accuracy of IT service delivery, ensuring that processes are executed in a standardized and reliable manner. Additionally, with automation, organizations can provide faster responses to service requests and incidents, improving the overall user experience.

Cloud computing has played a pivotal role in shaping the future of ITSM. The shift to the cloud has fundamentally changed how organizations manage their IT services. In traditional IT environments, services were typically hosted on physical infrastructure owned and managed by the organization. However, with the widespread adoption of cloud services, organizations now rely on third-party providers to deliver infrastructure, software, and platform services. This shift has introduced new challenges for ITSM, particularly around managing third-party relationships, ensuring service availability, and integrating cloud services with existing systems. ITSM frameworks must be adapted to manage hybrid environments, where both on-premise and cloud-based services are integrated. Effective capacity management, service level management, and incident response are crucial in these environments, as IT teams must coordinate with cloud providers to ensure that services meet performance standards and that any disruptions are addressed swiftly.

The increased reliance on digital technologies has also raised the importance of security and compliance in ITSM. As organizations collect and store more data, often in the cloud, they must ensure that their IT services comply with industry regulations and that sensitive data is protected. Security management has become a critical component of ITSM, with processes designed to ensure that services are secure, risks are managed, and compliance requirements are met. ITSM frameworks must incorporate robust security measures, such as identity and access management, data encryption, and incident response protocols, to mitigate the risk of cyberattacks and data breaches. In addition, IT teams must work closely with business units to understand regulatory requirements and ensure that IT services are designed to meet compliance standards. The integration of security management into ITSM practices ensures that digital transformation initiatives are not only efficient but also secure and compliant.

In the digital transformation era, user experience (UX) has also become a critical focus for ITSM. As organizations adopt more digital tools and platforms, the expectations of end-users have changed. Users now expect seamless, intuitive, and personalized experiences across all digital touchpoints. ITSM must evolve to meet these expectations, focusing on improving the user experience by providing faster response times, self-service options, and more proactive service delivery. IT teams can leverage data analytics to gain insights into user behavior, identify areas where service delivery can be improved, and tailor services to better meet user needs. This user-centric approach to ITSM ensures that digital transformation efforts not only improve internal processes but also enhance the experience for customers and employees.

As organizations undergo digital transformation, the traditional silos between IT and business units are becoming less relevant. Digital transformation requires a more integrated approach, where IT and business teams collaborate closely to ensure that technology supports strategic business goals. ITSM frameworks must be aligned with business processes to ensure that IT services are delivering the expected value to the business. This alignment allows IT teams to better understand business requirements, anticipate needs, and proactively deliver services that support business growth and innovation. Business and IT teams must work together to define service levels, measure performance, and make decisions about where to invest resources. This collaborative approach ensures that IT services are not only meeting operational needs but also contributing to the long-term success of the organization.

Furthermore, the rapid pace of digital transformation means that organizations must continuously adapt their ITSM practices to keep up with evolving technology trends. Emerging technologies such as artificial intelligence (AI), machine learning (ML), and the Internet of Things (IoT) are reshaping the IT landscape and creating new opportunities for organizations to improve service delivery. ITSM frameworks must be flexible enough to incorporate these technologies and leverage them to automate processes, improve decision-making, and enhance service delivery. For example, AI-powered chatbots can be used to handle simple service requests, freeing up IT staff to focus on more complex issues. Machine learning algorithms can be used to predict incidents and proactively address potential disruptions before they occur. By integrating these technologies into ITSM practices, organizations can stay ahead of the curve and deliver innovative services that meet the demands of the digital age.

In summary, ITSM in the digital transformation era requires a shift in mindset and approach to meet the challenges and opportunities posed by rapidly evolving technologies. The integration of ITSM with digital transformation initiatives enables organizations to deliver high-quality services that align with business needs, improve efficiency, and enhance the user experience. By embracing agility, automation, security, and collaboration, organizations can ensure that their IT services are responsive to the dynamic demands of the digital age while driving innovation and supporting business growth. As digital transformation continues to reshape industries, the role of ITSM will be crucial in ensuring that technology continues to deliver value, support business goals, and drive organizational success.

Customer Experience in ITSM

Customer experience (CX) has become one of the most significant factors for success in today's highly competitive market. As businesses increasingly rely on technology to deliver services, IT Service Management (ITSM) plays a critical role in shaping the overall experience of both internal users and external customers. The quality of IT services directly influences how customers perceive a company's ability to deliver on its promises, whether it's ensuring that an online service is always available, resolving technical issues quickly, or providing seamless access to information. In this context, ITSM is not only about ensuring that technology runs smoothly but also about optimizing every interaction that a customer or user has with IT services. As digital transformation continues to accelerate, the integration of customer experience into ITSM processes is essential for creating lasting, positive impressions that contribute to customer loyalty and business success.

The customer experience in ITSM is shaped by multiple touchpoints across various service management processes. From the moment a user submits a service request, encounters an incident, or seeks assistance with an issue, the responsiveness and efficiency of IT services are directly tied to the satisfaction of that individual. In a traditional IT environment, the primary focus was often on ensuring system uptime and technical performance. However, in the context of ITSM and customer experience, there is a shift towards a more holistic approach where IT teams must focus on how services are delivered to end-users and how those users interact with IT services at every step. The goal is to make these interactions as smooth, efficient, and pleasant as possible while also resolving issues promptly and accurately.

Effective customer experience in ITSM begins with understanding the needs, expectations, and pain points of customers, whether they are internal employees or external clients. Organizations need to recognize that customers expect high levels of service and support, and these expectations should be reflected in the service management processes. IT teams must not only address technical issues but also ensure that their interactions with customers are characterized by empathy, clarity, and efficiency. This requires training IT staff to communicate effectively with users, providing clear guidance during problem resolution, and setting realistic expectations about service delivery times.

A key aspect of improving customer experience within ITSM is implementing efficient and streamlined service request processes. When customers need IT support, they expect the process to be simple and effective. Service requests should be easy to submit, track, and resolve, and users should receive timely updates on the progress of their requests. One way to enhance this experience is by offering self-service portals that allow customers to resolve simple issues without having to contact IT staff directly. These portals can provide users with access to knowledge bases, FAQs, and automated troubleshooting tools, enabling them to resolve issues quickly and independently. The ability to solve problems on their own gives customers a sense of control and satisfaction, enhancing their overall experience with IT services.

Incident management also plays a vital role in shaping the customer experience. When an incident occurs—whether it's a system failure, software bug, or access issue—the speed at which it is addressed and resolved can significantly impact customer satisfaction. Customers expect their issues to be addressed promptly and effectively, and any delays or inefficiencies in the incident management process can lead to frustration. ITSM frameworks, such as ITIL, emphasize the importance of having structured incident management processes in place to ensure that issues are resolved as quickly as possible. By using tools to track, prioritize, and escalate incidents, IT teams can ensure that high-priority issues are addressed first and that customers are kept informed throughout the process. Clear communication and fast resolution not only minimize service disruption but also build trust between IT and the customer.

Problem management, though less visible than incident management, plays an equally important role in customer experience. While incident management addresses immediate disruptions, problem management works to identify and eliminate the root causes of recurring issues. When problems are not addressed at the root level, they can result in repeated incidents that frustrate users and hinder productivity. By proactively identifying and resolving underlying problems, ITSM ensures that customers experience fewer disruptions and that IT services remain reliable over time. This can be achieved by conducting root cause analysis for recurring incidents and implementing long-term fixes that prevent the same issues from arising in the future.

Another important aspect of customer experience in ITSM is the management of service levels. Service level agreements (SLAs) are used to define the expected performance standards for IT services, including response times, resolution times, and availability. Customers rely on these SLAs to know what to expect from the IT team, and ITSM processes must ensure that these expectations are consistently met. If SLAs are not met, customers can become dissatisfied, leading to a decline in their trust and confidence in the IT organization. To maintain a positive customer experience, it is essential that IT teams regularly monitor performance against SLAs, assess service delivery, and address any discrepancies that might impact the customer experience. Meeting or exceeding service levels reinforces customer confidence and satisfaction, ensuring that IT services contribute positively to the overall user experience.

In the context of cloud-based IT services, customer experience becomes even more critical as users often interact with services remotely and rely heavily on self-service options. The digital transformation of IT services means that users expect seamless access to cloud-based tools, applications, and data. ITSM processes must be adapted to ensure that these services are reliable, scalable, and user-friendly. Whether through automation, self-service portals, or enhanced monitoring, cloud services must be integrated with ITSM frameworks to ensure they meet the needs of customers while providing a consistent and high-quality experience. Ensuring that cloud services are continuously available, secure, and functioning properly is a key component of maintaining a positive customer experience.

User experience (UX) design is also an integral part of improving the customer experience in ITSM. IT teams must consider how users interact with IT systems, applications, and service portals. A well-designed user interface can make it easier for customers to submit service requests, report incidents, or find the information they need to resolve issues. The simpler and more intuitive the design, the more likely users are to engage with the IT services offered. UX design also plays a role in the overall satisfaction of users, as a smooth, easy-to-navigate experience enhances usability and reduces frustration.

As businesses continue to adopt more advanced technologies, such as artificial intelligence (AI) and machine learning (ML), the potential to improve customer experience in ITSM grows. AI-powered chatbots, for instance, can help users resolve common issues quickly by providing instant answers to frequently asked questions or guiding them through troubleshooting steps. ML algorithms can be used to predict incidents based on historical data, allowing IT teams to proactively address potential issues before they impact customers. These technologies enable a more personalized, efficient, and proactive approach to service delivery, which is essential for improving customer experience in a rapidly evolving digital landscape.

In summary, customer experience in ITSM is shaped by the quality, efficiency, and responsiveness of IT services. By focusing on processes such as incident management, problem management, service request fulfillment, and service level management, IT teams can ensure that they deliver high-quality services that meet the needs and expectations of their customers. Enhancing the customer experience requires an ongoing commitment to continuous improvement, proactive communication, and the integration of emerging technologies that enable faster, more efficient service delivery. Ultimately, by placing a strong emphasis on customer experience, organizations can ensure that their IT services support business objectives, enhance user satisfaction, and drive long-term success.

The Role of Automation in ITSM

Automation has become a central element in the transformation of IT Service Management (ITSM) in recent years. As businesses continue to grow in complexity and rely on more advanced technologies, the demands placed on IT services have increased. This has led to a growing need for IT departments to enhance their efficiency, reduce costs, and improve service delivery. One of the most effective ways to address these challenges is through the integration of automation into ITSM processes. Automation in ITSM can streamline operations, reduce human error, increase consistency, and allow IT teams to focus on more strategic tasks rather than repetitive manual work. The role of automation in ITSM is multifaceted and deeply integrated into several key processes, from incident management to service request fulfillment and change management.

One of the most prominent roles of automation in ITSM is its ability to improve the speed and efficiency of incident management. Incident management is one of the most critical functions within ITSM, as it deals with resolving IT service disruptions and ensuring that services are restored as quickly as possible. Traditionally, incident management involved manual processes, where IT teams had to diagnose issues, assign tickets, and follow up on the resolution. These processes often resulted in delays, inefficiencies, and a higher risk of human error. Automation changes this dynamic by allowing incidents to be logged, categorized, and prioritized automatically based on predefined rules. Automated systems can also assign tickets to the appropriate teams, send alerts, and even offer predefined solutions or troubleshooting steps to users. This significantly reduces response times, allowing IT teams to resolve issues more quickly and efficiently, while also providing users with faster solutions to their problems.

In addition to improving the speed of incident resolution, automation also enhances the consistency of incident management. With automated workflows, each incident is handled according to a consistent set of procedures, ensuring that no step is missed and that issues are addressed in the most effective way possible. Automation reduces the variation that can occur in manual processes, where different IT professionals might follow slightly different approaches to resolving the same type of issue. By standardizing the process, automation ensures that incidents are resolved more consistently, which in turn improves the overall quality of service delivery. It also helps ensure that incidents are resolved in accordance with service level agreements (SLAs), improving compliance with established targets.

Automation also plays a key role in improving the efficiency of service request management. In traditional ITSM models, users would submit service requests, which would then be manually reviewed, prioritized, and assigned to the appropriate service teams. The entire process could be time-consuming and prone to delays. With automation, much of this manual work can be eliminated. Self-service portals, for example, enable users to submit requests, search for solutions in knowledge bases, and even resolve certain types of requests on their own. Automated workflows can route requests to the right teams based on predefined criteria, ensuring that requests are handled more efficiently. Additionally, automated systems can track the progress of service requests, provide real-time updates to users, and notify IT teams when action is required. This leads to faster resolution times, improved user satisfaction, and reduced workloads for IT staff.

Another area where automation is transforming ITSM is in change management. Change management is crucial to maintaining the stability and reliability of IT services, especially in environments where frequent changes to systems, applications, and infrastructure are made. Traditionally, the change management process involved manual steps such as submitting change requests, reviewing them, obtaining approval, and tracking implementation progress. This process could be slow and cumbersome, particularly in large organizations with complex IT environments. Automation streamlines change management by automatically tracking change requests, ensuring that they are reviewed and approved according to predefined workflows, and scheduling changes based on availability and impact. Automated systems can also provide detailed reports on change implementation, allowing IT teams to track changes in real-time and quickly address any issues that arise. This level of automation not only improves the speed of change implementation but also ensures that changes are made in a controlled and systematic manner, reducing the risk of disruptions or errors.

Capacity management is another key area that benefits from automation. Effective capacity management ensures that IT services have the right amount of resources to meet current and future demand. Without automation, capacity planning can be a time-consuming process, requiring manual analysis of usage patterns, resource allocation, and demand forecasting. Automation allows for real-time monitoring of resource usage, helping IT teams identify potential bottlenecks or areas where additional resources are needed. Automated systems can also trigger alerts when capacity thresholds are reached, enabling proactive adjustments to be made before service disruptions occur. By automating capacity management, organizations can better align their resources with business needs, ensuring that services are always available and performing optimally.

Security management is an area where automation is increasingly important in ITSM. As cyber threats become more sophisticated and pervasive, it is essential that security measures are continuously monitored and enforced. Automation helps IT teams quickly identify potential security risks, such as unauthorized access attempts, vulnerabilities, or configuration errors, by continuously scanning systems and applications. Automated tools can generate alerts when suspicious activity is detected, allowing IT teams to respond swiftly to mitigate risks. Furthermore, automated patch management systems can ensure that systems are regularly updated with the latest security patches, reducing the risk of exploitation. By automating these processes, organizations can enhance their security posture and reduce the likelihood of data breaches or other security incidents.

Another significant advantage of automation in ITSM is the ability to generate and analyze data for continuous improvement. ITSM processes generate vast amounts of data, including incident logs, service request records, change management statistics, and performance metrics. With automation, this data can be collected and analyzed in real-time, providing valuable insights into service performance, trends, and areas for improvement. Automated reporting systems can identify recurring issues, inefficiencies in workflows, and areas where service levels are not being met. This allows IT teams to make data-driven decisions about process improvements, resource allocation, and service enhancements, ultimately leading to better service quality and higher user satisfaction.

Automation also facilitates greater scalability within ITSM. As organizations grow and their IT environments become more complex, managing an increasing volume of incidents, service requests, and changes can overwhelm manual processes. Automation enables ITSM systems to scale efficiently, handling larger volumes of work without requiring a proportional increase in staff. Automated workflows can handle routine tasks, allowing IT teams to focus on more strategic initiatives and problem-solving. This scalability is particularly important in organizations that are expanding their digital footprint or transitioning to cloud environments, where the complexity of managing IT services increases.

The integration of artificial intelligence (AI) and machine learning (ML) into ITSM further enhances the role of automation. AI can be used to automate decision-making processes, such as prioritizing incidents based on their impact or suggesting solutions to common problems. ML algorithms can analyze historical data to predict future incidents, identify patterns in service requests, and recommend preventive measures. This advanced form of automation can significantly improve the efficiency and effectiveness of ITSM processes, allowing IT teams to focus on high-value tasks while leaving routine decisions to AI-powered systems.

In summary, automation plays a transformative role in ITSM by enhancing efficiency, improving service delivery, and reducing the risk of errors. By automating key processes such as incident management, service request fulfillment, change management, capacity management, and security, organizations can streamline operations, improve service consistency, and ensure that IT services meet the demands of the business. The integration of AI and ML into ITSM further accelerates the benefits of automation, providing organizations with greater insight, agility, and scalability. As digital transformation continues to reshape the business landscape, automation will remain a key enabler of ITSM success, ensuring that IT services are optimized for the modern business environment.

Implementing ITSM: Challenges and Pitfalls

Implementing IT Service Management (ITSM) is a strategic initiative that many organizations pursue to enhance the quality, efficiency, and alignment of their IT services with business needs. ITSM frameworks, such as ITIL, provide well-defined processes and best practices for managing IT services across their lifecycle, from planning and design to delivery and improvement. However, despite the clear benefits that ITSM promises, the journey to successful implementation is often fraught with challenges and potential pitfalls. Organizations can face significant obstacles when attempting to integrate ITSM into their existing infrastructure, processes, and culture. Recognizing these challenges early and understanding how to navigate them is key to ensuring that ITSM delivers the expected value.

One of the most significant challenges in implementing ITSM is resistance to change. In many organizations, ITSM represents a significant shift in how IT services are managed and delivered. It often requires changes to established processes, workflows, and roles. Employees, especially those who are accustomed to existing practices, may be reluctant to adopt new methods, tools, and responsibilities. Resistance can come from various levels of the organization, from technical staff who are uncomfortable with new systems and workflows, to business leaders who may not fully understand the value of ITSM. Overcoming this resistance requires strong leadership, effective communication, and clear demonstrations of the benefits of ITSM. Change management strategies must be put in place to guide the organization through the transition, ensuring that all stakeholders understand the need for ITSM and are committed to its success.

Another challenge is the lack of alignment between IT and business objectives. ITSM is designed to improve the alignment of IT services with business needs, but achieving this alignment can be difficult. In many organizations, IT departments operate in silos, disconnected from the broader business strategy. This disconnect can result in IT services that do not fully meet the needs of the business or fail to support key objectives. Implementing ITSM successfully requires close collaboration between IT teams and business units to ensure that IT services are designed and delivered in a way that directly contributes to business success. Without this alignment, ITSM implementation can lead to inefficiencies, miscommunications, and missed opportunities for improvement. Bridging the gap between IT and business units is essential to ensure that IT services are not just technically sound, but also strategically relevant.

The complexity of existing IT environments can also pose significant challenges when implementing ITSM. Many organizations already have a wide range of IT systems, platforms, and tools in place, each with its own processes and procedures. Integrating these disparate systems into a unified ITSM framework can be a complex and time-consuming process. It often involves significant rework of existing workflows, as well as the adoption of new tools and technologies. In some cases, legacy systems may not be compatible with modern ITSM tools or may require significant customization to be integrated. This complexity can lead to delays in implementation, increased costs, and potential disruptions to service delivery. A clear roadmap and phased implementation plan can help mitigate these challenges, allowing the organization to make incremental changes while minimizing risk and disruption.

Resource constraints are another common pitfall in ITSM implementation. While the benefits of ITSM are well understood, many organizations underestimate the resources—both human and financial—required to implement and sustain an effective ITSM framework. Successful ITSM implementation requires dedicated personnel, proper training, and the investment in new technologies and tools. Without adequate resources, organizations may struggle to fully implement ITSM processes, leading to incomplete or ineffective deployment. Additionally, ongoing support and continuous improvement are essential for the long-term success of ITSM. Organizations must be prepared to allocate resources for regular training, process reviews, and system updates to ensure that the ITSM framework evolves in line with changing business needs. Failure to invest in these ongoing activities can result in stagnation, where the ITSM framework fails to deliver the expected results or becomes outdated.

The challenge of selecting the right tools and technologies is another hurdle in the ITSM implementation process. There is no one-size-fits-all solution for ITSM tools, as each organization has unique needs and requirements. Choosing the wrong tools can lead to inefficiencies, integration issues, and user frustration. It is important to carefully evaluate ITSM tools based on factors such as scalability, ease of integration with existing systems, and user experience. Additionally, organizations must ensure that they have the necessary infrastructure in place to support these tools, such as sufficient hardware, software, and network capacity. Implementing an ITSM tool without a proper understanding of the organization's requirements or technical environment can result in poor adoption rates and low return on investment. A well-defined requirements analysis and pilot testing phase can help mitigate these risks, ensuring that the chosen tools are a good fit for the organization.

Another common challenge in ITSM implementation is the ability to measure success. Implementing ITSM requires careful planning and monitoring, and organizations need to establish clear metrics and Key Performance Indicators (KPIs) to track progress. However, many organizations struggle to define meaningful metrics that accurately reflect the effectiveness of ITSM processes. Without the right metrics, it can be difficult to assess whether ITSM is delivering value or where improvements are needed. Effective measurement involves not only tracking service performance but also understanding the broader impact of ITSM on business outcomes. Establishing a baseline, setting clear goals, and regularly reviewing performance against these objectives are essential to ensuring that ITSM remains aligned with business priorities and continues to deliver measurable improvements.

Cultural and organizational factors also play a crucial role in the success or failure of ITSM implementation. Even with the right tools and processes in place, an organization's culture can significantly influence the success of ITSM adoption. In organizations where IT and business units are siloed, where there is a lack of collaboration, or where there is resistance to change, ITSM implementation can be slow and ineffective. Creating a culture of collaboration, transparency, and continuous improvement is essential for the successful adoption of ITSM. This requires leadership to foster an environment where IT and business teams work together toward shared goals and where employees are empowered to take ownership of the ITSM processes that affect their work.

Finally, a lack of executive support can hinder ITSM implementation. Successful ITSM adoption requires commitment from senior leadership to ensure that the necessary resources are allocated, the right priorities are set, and the organization as a whole is aligned with ITSM objectives. Without executive backing, ITSM initiatives are more likely to face resistance, be underfunded, or fail to gain the necessary traction. Senior leaders must champion the importance of ITSM, communicate its value to the organization, and ensure that ITSM becomes a core part of the company's strategic objectives. When leadership is engaged and supportive, ITSM implementation is more likely to succeed and deliver long-term benefits.

In summary, implementing ITSM involves overcoming a range of challenges, from resistance to change and misalignment with business goals to complexity in existing systems and resource constraints. However, by carefully planning the implementation process, ensuring the right tools and resources are in place, fostering a culture of collaboration, and securing executive support, organizations can successfully navigate these challenges. While the path to ITSM success may be difficult, the rewards in terms of improved service delivery, efficiency, and alignment with business objectives are well worth the effort.

ITSM Maturity Models

ITSM Maturity Models are frameworks designed to help organizations assess and improve the effectiveness of their IT Service Management (ITSM) practices. These models provide a structured approach to evaluating the maturity of an organization's ITSM processes, helping to identify areas for improvement, set goals, and track progress over time. The concept of maturity in ITSM refers to the level of sophistication and effectiveness of IT service management processes, practices, and organizational alignment with business needs. Maturity models offer a roadmap for organizations to evolve their ITSM capabilities, moving from basic, ad-hoc processes to more optimized, integrated, and strategic approaches. They provide organizations with a clear understanding of where they stand and what steps they need to take to reach higher levels of maturity.

The primary objective of an ITSM maturity model is to help organizations continuously improve their IT service management capabilities. By assessing their current state, organizations can gain valuable insights into the strengths and weaknesses of their ITSM processes, identify areas for improvement, and develop a roadmap for reaching more advanced stages of maturity. Maturity models help organizations to establish benchmarks, enabling them to measure progress over time and compare their performance with industry standards. Through this structured approach, organizations can ensure that their IT services are aligned with business objectives and that they are continuously optimizing their processes to deliver greater value.

Maturity models typically consist of several stages or levels, each representing a different degree of maturity. These stages range from an initial or basic level, where ITSM processes are informal and inconsistent, to a more advanced level, where processes are optimized, integrated, and continuously improved. In many models, the stages are described in terms of specific characteristics or capabilities that evolve over time. At the lowest level, an organization may have a reactive approach to IT service management, with limited process documentation and minimal standardization. As the organization matures, processes become more formalized, standardized, and aligned with business needs. Higher levels of maturity reflect a more proactive and strategic approach to ITSM, where processes are continuously improved, and IT services are closely integrated with business operations.

The first level of an ITSM maturity model is often referred to as the "initial" or "ad-hoc" stage. At this stage, organizations typically lack formalized ITSM processes and have minimal documentation or standardized procedures. IT services are managed reactively, meaning that issues are addressed only when they arise, rather than through proactive planning and management. This approach often leads to inconsistent service delivery, high levels of downtime, and inefficiencies in managing IT incidents and service requests. Organizations at this level may struggle with poor communication between IT and business units, and IT services may not be fully aligned with business goals. The focus is primarily on resolving immediate problems, with little emphasis on long-term improvement or planning.

As organizations progress through the maturity model, they move into the "repeatable" or "managed" stage. At this level, organizations begin to standardize their ITSM processes and establish more formalized procedures for managing incidents, changes, and service requests. There is a greater focus on service delivery, and organizations begin to implement tools and systems to help streamline operations. While the processes are still somewhat reactive, they are more structured and repeatable, leading to greater consistency in service delivery. IT teams at this stage typically start to measure key performance indicators (KPIs) and service levels, allowing them to track performance and identify areas for improvement. However, processes are still not fully integrated with business goals, and there may be gaps in the coordination between IT and business units.

At the "defined" or "proactive" stage, organizations have made significant strides in optimizing their ITSM processes. Processes are now standardized, documented, and aligned with industry best practices. There is a stronger emphasis on proactively managing IT services, with teams focusing on anticipating potential issues and taking preventative measures to avoid disruptions. ITSM processes are integrated across different functions, ensuring that service delivery is more cohesive and aligned with business needs. Organizations at this level also begin to establish clear service level agreements (SLAs) and conduct regular reviews to ensure that services meet the required performance standards. While the organization's IT services are more aligned with business goals, there is still room for improvement in terms of continuous service improvement and full integration with business operations.

The next level of maturity, often referred to as "managed" or "optimized," represents a more advanced stage of ITSM. At this stage, organizations have fully integrated their ITSM processes with business operations, and IT services are seen as a strategic enabler of business success. Processes are continuously measured and optimized for efficiency and effectiveness. Service delivery is highly proactive, with IT teams using advanced monitoring tools, predictive analytics, and automation to ensure that services are delivered seamlessly and without disruption. Organizations at this level are focused on continuous improvement, regularly assessing their performance and implementing changes to enhance service quality. IT teams work closely with business units to ensure that IT services are aligned with evolving business needs and that any potential issues are addressed before they impact the business. The focus is on delivering value to the business, with IT services optimized for performance, cost-effectiveness, and innovation.

The final level in most ITSM maturity models is the "optimized" or "innovative" stage. Organizations at this level have reached the highest degree of ITSM maturity. At this stage, IT services are not only fully integrated with business processes but are also driving innovation and digital transformation within the organization. IT teams work as strategic partners to the business, actively contributing to the organization's long-term goals and growth. Continuous improvement is ingrained in the organizational culture, and the focus is on leveraging emerging technologies, such as artificial intelligence (AI), machine learning (ML), and automation, to further optimize IT service delivery. Data-driven decision-making and advanced analytics are used to anticipate future business needs and optimize service management processes. IT is seen as a key enabler of business transformation, and organizations at this stage consistently deliver high-quality services that exceed customer expectations and support business objectives.

While maturity models provide a useful framework for assessing ITSM capabilities, organizations must be mindful of the challenges involved in moving through these stages. Progressing through the levels of maturity requires a significant investment of time, resources, and effort. Organizations may face resistance to change, particularly if there is a lack of understanding of the benefits of ITSM or if there is resistance from staff members who are accustomed to traditional ways of working. In addition, the complexity of implementing new tools, technologies, and processes can be overwhelming for some organizations. It is essential for organizations to adopt a phased approach to ITSM implementation, setting realistic goals and measuring progress incrementally. Gaining buy-in from key stakeholders, including executive leadership, is crucial for ensuring the success of the ITSM journey.

In the end, ITSM maturity models offer organizations a valuable tool for understanding their current state and developing a roadmap for improvement. By progressing through the stages of maturity, organizations can enhance their IT service delivery, increase operational efficiency, and align IT services with business goals. Although the journey to higher ITSM maturity may be challenging, the benefits in terms of improved service quality, greater agility, and enhanced business value make it a worthwhile endeavor.

Continuous Improvement in ITSM

Continuous improvement is a fundamental concept in IT Service Management (ITSM), driving the ongoing optimization of IT processes and services to align with business objectives and customer needs. The dynamic nature of modern IT environments, combined with the increasing demands of users and businesses, requires that IT services are not only reactive to issues but are actively enhanced over time. Continuous improvement within ITSM is essential for organizations aiming to maintain high service quality, reduce inefficiencies, and adapt to changing business and technological landscapes. By embedding a culture of continual service improvement (CSI), organizations can achieve greater operational efficiency, enhance user satisfaction, and ensure that their IT services remain aligned with evolving business goals.

At its core, continuous improvement in ITSM is about proactively identifying areas where IT services and processes can be enhanced to deliver greater value. It involves regularly assessing performance, identifying gaps or inefficiencies, and making incremental improvements to services, workflows, and processes. This philosophy is deeply embedded in ITSM frameworks such as ITIL, which emphasizes that service management is not a one-time task but a continuous cycle. ITSM frameworks provide structured methodologies and best practices that help organizations systematically assess and improve their IT services, ensuring that services remain responsive to changing needs and technologies.

One of the key principles of continuous improvement in ITSM is the use of data and metrics to inform decision-making. Organizations collect vast amounts of data related to service performance, incidents, service requests, and user feedback. This data provides valuable insights into how services are performing and where improvements are needed. By analyzing this data, IT teams can identify recurring issues, inefficiencies, and areas where service levels are not being met. For example, if incident resolution times are consistently longer than expected, IT teams can investigate the root causes and implement changes to streamline incident management processes. The use of metrics and data-driven decision-making helps organizations to identify problem areas, prioritize improvements, and measure the success of changes made to IT services.

A critical aspect of continuous improvement is feedback loops. In ITSM, feedback is essential for understanding the effectiveness of services and identifying areas for improvement. Feedback can come from a variety of sources, including end-users, business units, service desk agents, and performance monitoring tools. User feedback, in particular, is invaluable as it provides direct insights into the user experience and highlights areas where services may be falling short of expectations. Regular surveys, customer satisfaction ratings, and direct communication with users can reveal pain points in service delivery and help IT teams prioritize areas for improvement. Furthermore, feedback from internal IT teams can help identify bottlenecks or inefficiencies in service management processes that may not be immediately visible to end-users.

To facilitate continuous improvement, organizations must also adopt a structured approach to process management. ITSM frameworks such as ITIL encourage the use of process maturity models to assess the effectiveness of existing IT service management processes and to guide improvement efforts. These models provide a clear framework for evaluating where processes currently stand, identifying strengths and weaknesses, and determining the steps needed to achieve higher levels of maturity. By continuously assessing process maturity, organizations can ensure that their ITSM practices are evolving and that improvements are being made in a systematic and sustainable manner.

Change management is an integral part of continuous improvement in ITSM. Change is inevitable in any IT environment, and organizations must have robust processes in place to manage changes effectively. The change management process ensures that changes are implemented in a controlled manner to minimize disruption to services and users. However, continuous improvement within change management involves not only ensuring that changes are executed smoothly but also refining the process itself. By analyzing past changes, identifying lessons learned, and making adjustments to the change management process, organizations can reduce the risk of errors, improve response times, and enhance the overall efficiency of the process.

In addition to change management, problem management plays a critical role in continuous improvement. Problem management focuses on identifying the root causes of recurring incidents and implementing permanent solutions to prevent them from happening again. By conducting thorough root cause analyses and addressing the underlying issues, IT teams can reduce the frequency of incidents, improve service reliability, and enhance user satisfaction. Problem management is closely linked to incident management, and by continuously improving problem resolution processes, organizations can ensure that incidents are not only resolved quickly but also addressed at their source to prevent future disruptions.

Automation is another powerful tool for driving continuous improvement in ITSM. As organizations scale and service complexity increases, automation helps streamline repetitive tasks, reduce manual errors, and improve overall efficiency. IT teams can automate processes such as incident logging, ticket assignment, and service request fulfillment, freeing up valuable time and resources to focus on more strategic tasks. Automation also helps to ensure consistency in service delivery, as it eliminates human error and enforces standardized workflows. By incorporating automation into their ITSM practices, organizations can reduce the time required to complete routine tasks and enhance the speed and accuracy of service delivery.

Capacity management and performance monitoring also contribute to the continuous improvement cycle. As businesses grow and their IT needs evolve, capacity management ensures that IT resources are adequately scaled to meet demand. By continuously monitoring system performance and resource usage, organizations can anticipate potential issues and take proactive measures to avoid service disruptions. Performance monitoring tools provide real-time visibility into how IT services are performing, allowing IT teams to identify underperforming services or potential bottlenecks. This information can be used to optimize service delivery, reduce downtime, and improve the overall user experience.

Collaboration and communication across departments are essential for fostering continuous improvement in ITSM. ITSM is not just an IT function; it is a cross-functional effort that involves collaboration between IT teams, business units, and other stakeholders. Effective communication between IT and business leaders ensures that IT services are aligned with business needs and that improvement efforts are focused on delivering tangible value. Involving business units in the continuous improvement process helps IT teams understand the broader strategic goals of the organization and ensures that improvements are not made in isolation but are aligned with the overall business objectives.

Training and development are also critical components of continuous improvement in ITSM. As IT services and technologies evolve, IT teams must be equipped with the skills and knowledge required to manage these changes effectively. Regular training and professional development opportunities ensure that IT staff are up to date with the latest tools, techniques, and best practices in ITSM. By investing in the development of their teams, organizations can ensure that their ITSM processes remain effective and that they have the expertise necessary to drive ongoing improvement.

The journey of continuous improvement in ITSM is ongoing and ever-evolving. Organizations that adopt a mindset of continuous improvement ensure that their IT services remain aligned with the needs of the business, are responsive to user feedback, and are constantly evolving to meet new challenges and opportunities. By leveraging data, feedback, automation, and collaboration, organizations can continuously refine their ITSM processes, delivering higher-quality services and greater value to the business. As technology and business requirements continue to evolve, the ability to adapt and improve becomes a key competitive advantage in the modern digital landscape.

Building a Culture of Service Management

Building a culture of service management within an organization is an essential aspect of ensuring the long-term success and effectiveness of IT Service Management (ITSM) practices. A strong service management culture goes beyond merely implementing frameworks or processes; it requires a fundamental shift in the way that employees at all levels view and engage with IT services. For service management to be effective, it must be ingrained in the organization's values, practices, and everyday operations. This cultural shift demands the active involvement and commitment of leadership, clear communication throughout the organization, and the consistent application of service-oriented principles across both IT and business functions. Establishing a culture of service management creates an environment where continuous improvement, customer satisfaction, and collaboration are prioritized, ultimately leading to better service delivery and more efficient use of resources.

The foundation of a culture of service management is built on a shared understanding and appreciation of the value of IT services. For many organizations, IT has traditionally been seen as a technical support function, with limited interaction with the broader business strategy. However, in today's fast-paced and technology-driven world, IT services are central to the achievement of business objectives. In a service-oriented culture, the business does not view IT as a separate entity but as an integral partner that enables success. Employees across the organization must recognize that service management is not just the responsibility of the IT department but of everyone involved in delivering, using, or supporting IT services. This collective responsibility is essential to ensuring that IT services meet the needs of the business and provide value to end-users.

Leadership plays a pivotal role in building and nurturing a culture of service management. Without active buy-in and commitment from the top, it is difficult to embed service management principles into the fabric of the organization. Senior leaders must demonstrate a clear understanding of the importance of service management and actively promote its value to the organization. This includes aligning service management goals with business objectives and ensuring that resources are allocated to support service management initiatives. Leaders should also lead by example, championing a service-focused mindset and encouraging open communication between IT and business teams. When leadership prioritizes service management and exemplifies its core values, it sets the tone for the rest of the organization to follow.

Communication is another key component in cultivating a service management culture. Service management should not be perceived as a set of abstract processes or policies but as a practical approach to improving service delivery, meeting customer expectations, and driving business outcomes. This requires clear and consistent communication about the benefits of service management, the processes involved, and the role that each employee plays in contributing to its success. It is essential to communicate the goals of ITSM in a way that resonates with different stakeholders, from business units to IT staff, so they can understand how their actions contribute to achieving the overall service management objectives. By fostering a two-way communication channel, where feedback is encouraged and acted upon, organizations can ensure that service management practices are continuously aligned with evolving business needs.

One of the key challenges in building a culture of service management is overcoming resistance to change. Employees, especially those accustomed to traditional ways of working, may be reluctant to adopt new processes or mindsets. This resistance can stem from a lack of understanding of the benefits of service management or a perceived loss of control over existing processes. To address this challenge, organizations must invest in change management initiatives that clearly communicate the purpose and benefits of adopting service management principles. This includes providing training and support to employees at all levels, so they feel confident in their ability to contribute to service management goals. Additionally, it is important to involve employees early in the process, allowing them to provide input and voice concerns, thereby creating a sense of ownership and buy-in.

A service management culture also requires the establishment of clear processes and practices that support the delivery of high-quality IT services. This involves the implementation of frameworks such as ITIL, which provide a structured approach to managing IT services across their lifecycle. These frameworks outline best practices for incident management, change management, problem management, and other core ITSM processes. However, simply implementing these frameworks is not enough to build a strong service management culture. Organizations must also ensure that these processes are integrated into daily operations and supported by the appropriate tools, technologies, and resources. Service management should not be seen as an isolated set of processes but as an integral part of how the organization operates and delivers value to customers.

Furthermore, metrics and performance measurement play an essential role in building a culture of service management. Organizations must track and assess the performance of their IT services and service management processes to ensure that they are delivering the desired outcomes. This involves establishing key performance indicators (KPIs) that align with the organization's goals and using data to monitor progress. Regular performance reviews provide opportunities to identify areas for improvement and recognize successes. A culture of continuous improvement is vital in service management, and the use of metrics helps drive this culture by providing the necessary feedback to inform decisions and refine processes. By fostering an environment where performance is regularly evaluated and improvements are encouraged, organizations can continuously evolve their service management practices to meet changing business and customer demands.

Another essential element in building a culture of service management is the focus on customer-centricity. In a service management culture, the customer—whether internal or external—should always be at the center of IT service delivery. IT teams should strive to understand the needs and expectations of users and ensure that services are designed and delivered to meet these needs. Regular engagement with customers, such as through surveys, feedback sessions, or user experience studies, helps organizations understand how services are perceived and where improvements can be made. A customer-centric approach helps foster trust and loyalty, as users feel that their needs are understood and prioritized. Additionally, it ensures that IT services are not only functional but also aligned with business goals, ultimately contributing to the success of the organization.

In addition to customer focus, collaboration and teamwork across different departments are vital for fostering a culture of service management. IT services are not isolated; they are intricately connected with various other functions, from HR and finance to operations and customer support. Service management should be a cross-functional effort, where different teams collaborate to deliver seamless services that meet business and user needs. Breaking down silos and encouraging cross-departmental collaboration fosters a sense of shared responsibility for service quality. When different teams work together with a service-oriented mindset, the entire organization benefits from improved efficiency, smoother workflows, and better service delivery.

Lastly, recognition and reward systems are essential for reinforcing the service management culture. Employees should be recognized and rewarded for their contributions to improving service delivery, whether it's through successfully resolving incidents, identifying improvements in processes, or collaborating across teams. Recognition encourages a positive attitude toward service management and motivates employees to continue improving their performance. Celebrating small wins and acknowledging the efforts of individuals and teams helps to build momentum and reinforces the importance of service management as a key business priority.

Building a culture of service management requires a comprehensive approach that encompasses leadership, communication, process alignment, and a focus on customer needs. It is not a one-time initiative but an ongoing effort that requires continuous investment, adaptation, and commitment from all levels of the organization. When successfully implemented, a strong service management culture leads to improved service quality, greater operational efficiency, and enhanced customer satisfaction, ultimately driving the overall success of the business.

ITSM Governance and Compliance

Governance and compliance are critical components of IT Service Management (ITSM), ensuring that IT services are aligned with business goals, regulations, and industry standards while maintaining the effectiveness and efficiency of service delivery. In today's increasingly complex and regulated IT environment, organizations must not only focus on delivering quality services but also adhere to stringent governance frameworks and compliance requirements. The role of governance in ITSM is to establish the structure, processes, and controls necessary to ensure that IT services are delivered in a way that supports business objectives and meets legal, regulatory, and contractual obligations. Compliance, on the other hand, ensures that these services adhere to external laws and industry-specific standards, safeguarding the organization from potential risks associated with non-compliance.

The concept of governance in ITSM involves defining clear roles, responsibilities, and accountabilities within the organization. It ensures that there is oversight of IT service delivery and that decisions regarding service management processes are made in alignment with the organization's overall strategy. Effective governance in ITSM requires a well-defined organizational structure where senior leaders, such as the Chief Information Officer (CIO) and IT managers, are responsible for setting strategic objectives, while operational teams focus on delivering services in line with those goals. This structure ensures that all ITSM processes, such as incident management, change management, and service level management, are consistently followed and aligned with the organization's long-term vision.

A key element of ITSM governance is the establishment of policies, procedures, and standards that guide the delivery of IT services. These policies provide a framework for decision-making, ensuring that IT services are managed in a consistent and controlled manner. For example, change management policies define the procedures for requesting, approving, and implementing changes to IT systems, ensuring that changes are made in a controlled manner that minimizes disruption to services. Similarly, service level management policies outline the expectations for service delivery and the processes for monitoring and reporting on service performance. These policies and procedures are integral to maintaining consistency and ensuring that services meet the required standards of quality, availability, and security.

In addition to policies and procedures, ITSM governance also involves establishing performance metrics and key performance indicators (KPIs) to track the effectiveness of service management processes. By measuring performance against predefined targets, organizations can assess whether their IT services are meeting business requirements and identify areas for improvement. Governance ensures that these metrics are used to drive decision-making, enabling the organization to optimize service delivery and improve overall efficiency. Regular reviews of these metrics allow organizations to identify trends, uncover inefficiencies, and take corrective actions when necessary. This data-driven approach to governance ensures that IT services continuously evolve to meet changing business needs.

Compliance, as part of ITSM, is about ensuring that the organization's IT services meet the legal, regulatory, and contractual requirements that apply to its industry. Different industries are subject to different sets of regulations, and non-compliance can lead to significant legal, financial, and reputational risks. For example, organizations in the healthcare industry must comply with regulations like the Health Insurance Portability and Accountability Act (HIPAA), which sets standards for protecting patient data. Similarly, financial institutions must adhere to regulations such as the Sarbanes-Oxley Act (SOX) to ensure transparency in financial reporting. ITSM plays a critical role in ensuring that IT services are compliant with these regulations, particularly in areas such as data security, privacy, and reporting.

To achieve compliance, ITSM frameworks must incorporate processes and controls that ensure the security and integrity of data, as well as the proper documentation and reporting of service activities. This includes the implementation of data protection measures, such as encryption, access controls, and secure communication protocols, to safeguard sensitive information. ITSM frameworks also help organizations track and document changes to IT systems, ensuring that the necessary approvals are in place and that all changes are made in compliance with regulatory requirements. Additionally, ITSM processes support auditability, enabling organizations to demonstrate compliance during regulatory audits or internal reviews.

One of the key challenges in ITSM governance and compliance is managing the complexity of evolving regulations and standards. As technology continues to advance, new compliance requirements and industry standards emerge, requiring organizations to continuously update their ITSM processes and controls. For example, the introduction of the General Data Protection Regulation (GDPR) in the European Union has imposed new requirements on how organizations handle personal data. Similarly, the increasing use of cloud computing and third-party services introduces additional compliance considerations, particularly around data residency, security, and access control. Governance in ITSM must be flexible enough to adapt to these changes, ensuring that the organization's IT services remain compliant with current regulations and best practices.

Effective governance and compliance in ITSM also require close collaboration between IT and other business functions. IT departments are often responsible for implementing and maintaining compliance processes, but other areas of the organization, such as legal, finance, and human resources, may also play a role in ensuring compliance. By fostering cross-functional collaboration, organizations can ensure that compliance requirements are understood and applied across all areas of the business. This collaboration is particularly important when dealing with complex regulations, as it ensures that all relevant stakeholders are involved in decision-making and that compliance requirements are properly addressed in IT service delivery.

Risk management is another critical component of governance and compliance in ITSM. IT services are exposed to various risks, including cybersecurity threats, data breaches, and system failures, all of which can have significant legal, financial, and reputational consequences. Effective governance helps identify, assess, and mitigate these risks by implementing appropriate controls and processes to safeguard IT services. ITSM processes such as incident management, problem management, and security management are all designed to help organizations manage and reduce risk. By identifying and addressing risks proactively, organizations can prevent compliance violations and minimize the impact of security incidents or service disruptions.

Governance and compliance in ITSM are not static; they must be continuously monitored and refined to ensure that they remain effective. Regular audits and assessments are essential for evaluating the effectiveness of governance processes and ensuring that compliance requirements are being met. These audits can help identify weaknesses in existing policies and procedures, providing organizations with an opportunity to make improvements before compliance issues arise. Additionally, organizations must stay informed about changes in the regulatory landscape and adjust their ITSM practices accordingly. This proactive approach to governance and compliance ensures that organizations can manage their IT services in a way that minimizes risk and aligns with both business and regulatory requirements.

In conclusion, ITSM governance and compliance are integral to the successful delivery of IT services that meet both business objectives and regulatory standards. Governance provides the framework for managing IT services, ensuring that they are delivered in a controlled and consistent manner, while compliance ensures that these services meet legal and industry requirements. Together, governance and compliance help organizations mitigate risks, improve service quality, and align IT with business needs. As regulatory environments continue to evolve, ITSM must remain flexible and adaptive to ensure that organizations maintain effective governance and compliance in the face of new challenges.

ITSM Best Practices

IT Service Management (ITSM) best practices refer to the processes, procedures, and strategies that organizations adopt to ensure that their IT services are delivered in a consistent, efficient, and effective manner. These best practices are based on industry standards and frameworks, such as ITIL (Information Technology Infrastructure Library), COBIT (Control Objectives for Information and Related Technologies), and others, which provide structured guidance for managing IT services throughout their lifecycle. The adoption of ITSM best practices is crucial for organizations aiming to optimize their IT operations, enhance service delivery, improve customer satisfaction, and ensure alignment with business objectives.

One of the foundational principles of ITSM best practices is the alignment of IT services with the needs of the business. IT is no longer seen as a support function but as a key enabler of business success. As businesses evolve and become increasingly reliant on technology, IT services must be designed and delivered to support business goals effectively. Best practices in ITSM focus on ensuring that IT services are not only technically sound but also meet the strategic and operational requirements of the business. This requires a deep understanding of the business processes and objectives, as well as clear communication between IT teams and business leaders to ensure that IT services are aligned with the overall direction of the organization.

A critical aspect of ITSM best practices is the use of standardized processes to manage IT services. Standardization is essential for ensuring consistency and reliability in service delivery. Best practices emphasize the importance of defining, documenting, and following established processes for key IT service management areas, including incident management, change management, problem management, service level management, and service request fulfillment. By following standardized processes, organizations can reduce the likelihood of errors, improve service quality, and ensure that services are delivered in a consistent and predictable manner. This also facilitates better communication and collaboration among IT teams, as everyone follows the same set of procedures and understands their roles and responsibilities within the service delivery framework.

Another key best practice in ITSM is the emphasis on continuous improvement. IT services are dynamic, and the needs of the business and users evolve over time. As such, it is essential for organizations to continuously assess their IT services and processes to identify areas for improvement. ITSM best practices encourage the use of performance metrics and key performance indicators (KPIs) to measure service delivery and identify inefficiencies or gaps. Regular reviews of service performance allow organizations to make data-driven decisions and implement changes that enhance service quality, reduce costs, and improve overall efficiency. Continuous improvement is not only about addressing problems but also about proactively seeking opportunities to optimize IT services, streamline processes, and adopt new technologies that support the business.

A customer-centric approach is another critical component of ITSM best practices. In today's highly competitive environment, the satisfaction of end-users and customers is paramount. Best practices in ITSM emphasize the importance of understanding customer needs and ensuring that IT services meet or exceed their expectations. IT teams must be responsive to customer requests, handle incidents and service requests promptly, and ensure that services are delivered with high quality and reliability. Regular customer feedback, whether through surveys, service reviews, or direct interactions, is essential for understanding how well IT services are meeting customer needs and where improvements can be made. By placing the customer at the center of IT service delivery, organizations can enhance customer satisfaction and build stronger relationships with both internal and external users.

ITSM best practices also focus on proactive management of IT services. While traditional IT management often took a reactive approach to service disruptions, modern ITSM practices emphasize the importance of anticipating and preventing issues before they occur. This proactive approach includes the use of monitoring tools to track the performance of IT systems, identify potential problems, and take corrective actions before they impact service availability or performance. In areas like change management, best practices advocate for thorough impact assessments and testing before implementing changes to minimize the risk of disruption. By being proactive in service management, organizations can reduce downtime, improve service reliability, and provide a more seamless experience for users.

Another best practice in ITSM is the use of service-level agreements (SLAs) to define clear expectations for service delivery. SLAs are formal agreements between IT and business units that outline the expected levels of service in terms of availability, response times, resolution times, and other key metrics. SLAs provide a framework for measuring service performance and help ensure that IT services meet the needs of the business. Best practices recommend that SLAs be specific, measurable, and aligned with business priorities to ensure that both IT teams and business units have a clear understanding of what is expected. Regular monitoring and reporting on SLA performance allow organizations to track whether service levels are being met and identify areas where improvements are needed.

In addition to SLAs, effective communication is a fundamental ITSM best practice. IT teams must communicate clearly and regularly with both business units and end-users to ensure that everyone is aware of service status, changes, and any issues that may arise. Communication during incidents and service disruptions is particularly important, as users need to be informed about the status of their requests and any actions being taken to resolve the issue. Transparency and timely communication help build trust with users and reduce frustration during service interruptions. Furthermore, IT teams must communicate the value of ITSM processes and initiatives to the broader organization, ensuring that stakeholders understand how IT services contribute to the achievement of business goals.

Governance is another essential element of ITSM best practices. Effective governance ensures that IT services are managed in a controlled, consistent, and accountable manner. This includes defining roles and responsibilities, establishing decision-making frameworks, and implementing policies and procedures that guide IT service management processes. Governance also involves regular audits and reviews to ensure that ITSM practices are being followed and that services are being delivered in accordance with organizational standards and regulatory requirements. Strong governance ensures that IT services are managed in a way that minimizes risk, optimizes performance, and supports business objectives.

The use of automation is increasingly recognized as a key best practice in ITSM. As IT environments become more complex and the demand for services grows, automation helps organizations streamline their processes, reduce manual errors, and improve efficiency. Best practices in ITSM recommend the automation of routine tasks, such as incident logging, ticket assignment, service request fulfillment, and reporting. Automation not only speeds up service delivery but also ensures consistency and accuracy in the execution of tasks. By incorporating automation into their ITSM processes, organizations can reduce the burden on IT staff, allowing them to focus on more strategic activities and deliver higher-value services to the business.

Finally, ITSM best practices highlight the importance of alignment between IT and business objectives. IT services must not only be efficient and reliable but also closely aligned with the strategic goals of the organization. Best practices recommend that IT teams work closely with business units to understand their needs, priorities, and challenges. This alignment ensures that IT services are not only technically sound but also add value to the business and support its growth. By aligning IT services with business objectives, organizations can ensure that their IT investments deliver the maximum return and contribute to overall business success.

In the end, ITSM best practices provide a comprehensive framework for managing IT services in a way that supports business goals, improves service quality, and enhances customer satisfaction. By following these best practices, organizations can streamline their IT operations, reduce inefficiencies, and create a culture of continuous improvement that drives ongoing success. As the business and technological landscape continues to evolve, the adoption of ITSM best practices remains essential for ensuring that IT services are delivered with consistency, reliability, and value.

The Future of ITSM Frameworks

The landscape of IT Service Management (ITSM) is undergoing significant transformations as organizations seek to adapt to the rapidly evolving demands of technology, business, and customer expectations. ITSM frameworks, which have traditionally been grounded in structured processes and well-established methodologies, are now being reshaped to meet the challenges of modern digital environments. As cloud computing, artificial intelligence (AI), automation, and DevOps continue to dominate the IT landscape, ITSM frameworks must evolve to keep pace with these changes. The future of ITSM frameworks will be defined by their ability to embrace agility, leverage emerging technologies, and integrate with business objectives, all while maintaining a focus on delivering value to users and customers.

One of the key trends shaping the future of ITSM is the increasing demand for agility. Traditional ITSM frameworks, such as ITIL, were designed to establish control and consistency over IT service delivery, focusing on minimizing risks, ensuring stability, and maintaining service levels. However, in the fast-moving world of digital transformation, organizations are looking for ways to be more responsive to change and innovation. Agility in ITSM means the ability to rapidly adjust to shifting business needs, customer demands, and technological advances. The future of ITSM will likely involve a greater emphasis on lightweight, flexible frameworks that can be customized to meet the specific needs of different organizations, rather than adhering rigidly to one-size-fits-all methodologies. IT teams will increasingly need to implement ITSM practices that support fast-paced innovation and iterative development, such as integrating ITSM processes with agile methodologies and DevOps practices.

Another critical shift in the future of ITSM frameworks is the growing reliance on automation. As organizations seek to improve the efficiency and speed of service delivery, automation will play a pivotal role in streamlining routine tasks and processes. AI-driven automation, machine learning, and robotic process automation (RPA) will increasingly be integrated into ITSM frameworks, allowing organizations to automate repetitive tasks such as incident resolution, service requests, and change management workflows. This will enable IT teams to focus on more complex and strategic activities, such as problem management and continuous improvement, while ensuring that day-to-day operations run smoothly and efficiently. Additionally, automation will help reduce human error, improve service consistency, and ensure that IT services meet the defined service levels without the need for constant manual intervention.

The integration of artificial intelligence and machine learning into ITSM frameworks will continue to evolve, enhancing decision-making, predictive analytics, and problem resolution. AI will be used to analyze vast amounts of data generated by IT systems, helping IT teams identify trends, anticipate potential issues, and make informed decisions. For example, AI algorithms can predict potential incidents based on historical data and proactively resolve issues before they impact users. Chatbots and virtual assistants powered by AI will also play a greater role in enhancing user experience, providing instant support for routine requests, and guiding users through troubleshooting steps. This integration of AI into ITSM will improve the speed, efficiency, and accuracy of service delivery, while also reducing the burden on IT support teams.

Another significant change in the future of ITSM frameworks is the increasing focus on the integration of IT services with business processes. As organizations strive to become more digitally connected and aligned with customer expectations, IT services must be seamlessly integrated into the broader business context. The future of ITSM frameworks will likely involve a closer collaboration between IT teams and business units, where IT services are viewed not just as a support function but as a key enabler of business outcomes. This requires ITSM frameworks to be more adaptive, flexible, and closely aligned with business goals, with a focus on delivering tangible value to the organization. IT teams will need to have a deeper understanding of the business processes they support and ensure that IT services are optimized to meet both current and future business needs. This alignment will help ensure that IT is seen as a strategic asset and not just a cost center.

In addition to the integration with business processes, the future of ITSM frameworks will also see an increased emphasis on service experience. As customers become more accustomed to seamless, high-quality digital experiences, organizations will need to deliver IT services that meet these expectations. This includes providing fast, reliable, and personalized service that is tailored to the needs of users. The future of ITSM frameworks will focus more on customer experience (CX) and user experience (UX), with ITSM processes evolving to prioritize the end-user's journey. This might include self-service portals, mobile access, and proactive service delivery models that anticipate user needs before they arise. With service experience becoming a central component of ITSM, IT teams will be expected to monitor and improve service delivery continuously, using data and feedback to refine processes and enhance the user experience.

Security and compliance will remain central to ITSM frameworks, but the future will bring new challenges as the regulatory landscape becomes more complex. Organizations will need to ensure that their IT services comply with a growing array of regulations, such as data privacy laws and industry-specific standards, while also addressing cybersecurity threats that are becoming increasingly sophisticated. ITSM frameworks will need to incorporate advanced security management processes that ensure the integrity, confidentiality, and availability of data and services. As cyber threats continue to evolve, ITSM frameworks will need to integrate more robust security measures, including continuous monitoring, risk assessments, and real-time threat detection. Compliance will also need to be built into every aspect of the ITSM lifecycle, with automated systems ensuring that services are consistently aligned with regulatory requirements and that any deviations are immediately flagged and addressed.

The growing trend toward hybrid and multi-cloud environments will also impact the future of ITSM frameworks. Organizations are increasingly adopting cloud technologies to improve scalability, flexibility, and cost-efficiency, but this introduces new challenges for managing IT services across different environments. The future of ITSM will involve frameworks that are designed to support hybrid IT infrastructures, where on-premise, private cloud, and public cloud services are integrated and managed cohesively. This will require new tools and processes for monitoring and managing services across multiple platforms, ensuring that services are delivered consistently regardless of where they are hosted. Additionally, as organizations rely more on third-party vendors and service providers, ITSM frameworks will need to be adapted to manage vendor relationships and ensure that service levels are met across external providers.

Collaboration between IT teams and business stakeholders will become more essential in shaping the future of ITSM frameworks. As organizations move towards a more integrated approach to IT and business operations, ITSM will need to evolve to reflect this changing relationship. IT teams will need to work closely with business units to understand their needs, set priorities, and co-create IT services that deliver value. This will require a cultural shift where IT is seen as a partner to the business, not just a provider of technology. ITSM frameworks will need to facilitate this collaboration by enabling clear communication, shared goals, and transparency in service delivery.

In the future, ITSM frameworks will be more agile, data-driven, and closely aligned with business outcomes. The ability to integrate emerging technologies, adapt to changing business needs, and focus on the overall service experience will be essential for organizations that wish to stay competitive. ITSM will no longer be a set of static processes but a dynamic, continuous process of improvement, ensuring that IT services are optimized to meet the ever-evolving demands of the business and its customers. The future of ITSM frameworks will be characterized by innovation, flexibility, and a deeper integration with business objectives, ensuring that IT remains a strategic driver of success.

The Role of AI and Machine Learning in ITSM

The integration of Artificial Intelligence (AI) and Machine Learning (ML) into IT Service Management (ITSM) is revolutionizing how IT services are delivered, managed, and optimized. As technology continues to advance, AI and ML offer unprecedented opportunities to enhance efficiency, improve decision-making, and deliver more personalized and responsive services to users. These technologies are transforming traditional ITSM processes, making them more proactive, predictive, and automated. The role of AI and ML in ITSM is expanding beyond simple automation tasks, becoming integral to improving service delivery, reducing operational costs, and creating more agile IT environments.

AI and ML are particularly valuable in the realm of incident management, a core component of ITSM. Traditionally, when incidents occurred, IT teams had to manually categorize, prioritize, and assign them to the appropriate personnel. This process, while effective, was often time-consuming and subject to human error. AI, however, can streamline this process by automatically categorizing and prioritizing incidents based on predefined criteria and historical data. Through natural language processing (NLP), AI can analyze incoming incident reports, understand the context, and categorize them with a high degree of accuracy. Furthermore, ML algorithms can analyze historical data to predict the likelihood of incident escalation, helping IT teams respond more effectively before problems worsen. This predictive capability allows IT teams to proactively address issues, reducing downtime and improving overall service availability.

In addition to incident management, AI and ML play a critical role in problem management. Problem management involves identifying the root causes of recurring incidents and implementing long-term solutions to prevent their reoccurrence. In traditional ITSM environments, this process was often reactive and based on manual analysis of incidents and service disruptions. AI and ML change this dynamic by enabling more proactive problem management. Machine learning models can identify patterns in large datasets, detecting recurring issues that may not be immediately apparent. By analyzing trends and correlations across different incidents, ML algorithms can uncover root causes and recommend solutions more efficiently. This enables IT teams to resolve underlying issues faster, improving service reliability and reducing the frequency of incidents.

Another area where AI and ML are making significant contributions to ITSM is in change management. Managing changes to IT systems and infrastructure is a complex and risky process that requires careful planning, testing, and execution. AI and ML can help mitigate the risks associated with change management by predicting the impact of proposed changes before they are implemented. Machine learning algorithms can analyze historical data on previous changes, identify potential conflicts or issues, and provide insights into the most effective change management strategies. AI can also assist in automating parts of the change approval process, ensuring that changes are executed in a controlled and timely manner. This reduces the likelihood of service disruptions caused by poorly planned or executed changes and improves the overall efficiency of change management.

AI and ML are also transforming service request management by enabling more efficient handling of service requests and reducing the burden on IT support teams. Traditionally, service requests were handled manually, with support teams responding to each request individually, often following repetitive procedures. AI can automate many of these tasks, such as handling common service requests or providing users with answers to frequently asked questions through chatbots or virtual assistants. Machine learning algorithms can also analyze past service requests and identify trends, helping IT teams predict and proactively address recurring user needs. This level of automation not only improves response times but also allows IT teams to focus on more complex or high-priority requests, enhancing the overall service experience for end-users.

The use of AI and ML in ITSM is also enabling the creation of self-healing systems. These systems can automatically detect and resolve certain types of issues without human intervention. For example, if a server starts to show signs of performance degradation, AI-powered monitoring tools can identify the issue and initiate corrective actions, such as reallocating resources or restarting services. In more advanced scenarios, ML algorithms can learn from past incidents and apply this knowledge to predict and prevent future problems. This shift towards self-healing systems not only reduces the workload on IT teams but also improves service availability and minimizes the impact of service disruptions on end-users.

AI and ML are also enhancing decision-making within ITSM processes. One of the challenges of traditional ITSM is the reliance on historical data and manual analysis to make decisions about service improvements, resource allocation, and priority setting. With AI and ML, IT teams can make data-driven decisions based on real-time analysis of service performance, user feedback, and historical trends. For example, AI can analyze large volumes of data to identify bottlenecks in IT service delivery, recommend optimizations to improve efficiency, and suggest ways to better allocate resources. ML algorithms can also help IT teams forecast future demand for IT services, enabling them to proactively scale resources and ensure that services remain responsive to user needs.

Moreover, AI and ML are improving the overall user experience by enabling more personalized IT services. Through the use of AI-driven analytics, IT teams can gain deeper insights into how users interact with IT services, what their preferences are, and where they face difficulties. This information can be used to tailor IT services to meet the specific needs of individual users or business units. For example, AI can suggest personalized IT resources or services based on a user's historical behavior and preferences. This personalization improves user satisfaction, increases engagement with IT services, and helps ensure that users have access to the resources they need to be productive.

Furthermore, the integration of AI and ML into ITSM frameworks enhances the efficiency of service management by reducing manual intervention and streamlining processes. By automating routine tasks, such as ticket categorization, service request fulfillment, and incident resolution, AI frees up valuable time for IT support staff to focus on more complex tasks that require human expertise. Automation also ensures that processes are executed consistently, reducing the risk of errors and improving the quality of service delivery. As AI and ML technologies continue to evolve, the scope of automation in ITSM will expand, allowing for even greater efficiency and productivity within IT teams.

The future of AI and ML in ITSM is poised to bring even more transformative changes. As AI technologies continue to advance, their ability to learn, adapt, and provide deeper insights will enable organizations to continuously improve their ITSM practices. AI and ML will continue to reduce the reliance on manual processes, improve the accuracy of decision-making, and create more personalized and responsive IT services. By harnessing the power of AI and ML, organizations can drive efficiencies, enhance user experiences, and better align their IT services with the needs of the business, ultimately improving the value that IT delivers to the organization.

Incorporating AI and machine learning into ITSM processes not only drives operational efficiencies but also allows for a shift toward more intelligent, predictive, and user-centered IT services. The future of ITSM, supported by AI and ML, will be characterized by greater autonomy, faster response times, and a more agile approach to service management, ensuring that IT services can meet the ever-changing demands of both businesses and their customers.

ITSM in Large Enterprises vs. Small Businesses

The application of IT Service Management (ITSM) varies significantly between large enterprises and small businesses due to differences in organizational size, complexity, resources, and business needs. While both large enterprises and small businesses recognize the importance of ITSM in ensuring the effective delivery of IT services, their approaches to adopting and implementing ITSM practices are often shaped by these structural and resource-based disparities. Understanding the distinct challenges and opportunities faced by each type of organization in adopting ITSM can provide valuable insights into how ITSM frameworks, such as ITIL, can be tailored to fit the unique requirements of each.

In large enterprises, the sheer scale and complexity of IT operations necessitate a more structured and formal approach to ITSM. These organizations often have sprawling IT environments with a wide array of systems, applications, and services that need to be managed and optimized. This complexity requires a comprehensive and standardized set of processes to ensure that IT services are delivered efficiently, meet user expectations, and align with business goals. Large enterprises typically implement ITSM frameworks, such as ITIL, in a way that is deeply embedded in the organization's operations, often involving the creation of specific roles and departments dedicated to managing IT services. These organizations can afford to invest in sophisticated ITSM tools, process automation, and dedicated IT staff to handle the intricacies of service delivery, incident management, change management, and problem resolution.

The need for standardized and scalable processes in large enterprises is evident across all ITSM functions. For example, in incident management, large enterprises often rely on ITSM tools to automate the categorization, prioritization, and resolution of incidents, ensuring that service disruptions are handled swiftly and in accordance with established service level agreements (SLAs). Similarly, change management in large enterprises is often a highly structured process, involving rigorous approval workflows, impact assessments, and testing protocols to ensure that changes to IT systems are executed with minimal disruption to business operations. These organizations often require a large team of IT staff to support these processes and manage the coordination across multiple departments, regions, and business units. ITSM in large enterprises is, therefore, characterized by a high degree of centralization, standardization, and coordination.

On the other hand, small businesses face a very different set of circumstances when it comes to ITSM. With fewer resources, smaller IT teams, and less complex IT environments, small businesses often need to adopt a more flexible and lightweight approach to service management. The focus in small businesses is often on delivering IT services that are responsive and cost-effective, rather than implementing the highly standardized and structured processes seen in larger organizations. Small businesses may not have the same level of dedicated IT staff or specialized ITSM tools, meaning that their ITSM practices are typically more informal and less process-heavy. In many cases, ITSM in small businesses is driven by the need to address immediate service issues rather than proactively managing a comprehensive IT service delivery framework.

The flexibility of small businesses can also be a significant advantage when it comes to adopting ITSM. Without the layers of bureaucracy and complex organizational structures found in large enterprises, small businesses can often make quicker decisions and implement ITSM practices more rapidly. For example, in the area of incident management, small businesses might rely on a more hands-on approach, with IT staff directly addressing service disruptions and providing support to end-users in real-time. While this approach may not be as formal or systematic as that of a large enterprise, it can be effective in ensuring that critical issues are resolved promptly, particularly in environments where IT systems are less complex.

Despite these differences, there are common challenges faced by both large enterprises and small businesses in implementing ITSM. One of the primary challenges for both is ensuring that IT services are aligned with business objectives. Whether in a large enterprise or a small business, ITSM practices must be designed to support the organization's goals and priorities. In large enterprises, this often means ensuring that IT services are optimized for different departments and business units, whereas, in small businesses, it involves tailoring IT services to meet the needs of a more limited user base. For both types of organizations, the focus must be on delivering value to the business, whether through optimizing resources, improving efficiency, or enhancing customer experience.

Another challenge common to both large enterprises and small businesses is the need for continuous improvement. In large enterprises, this is often driven by formal reviews, performance metrics, and ongoing optimization of ITSM processes. In small businesses, continuous improvement may be more informal, with IT staff continually assessing service performance and making adjustments as needed. However, the principles of continuous improvement are important in both settings, as organizations must regularly assess their IT services, identify areas for optimization, and implement changes that enhance service delivery.

One of the key differences between large enterprises and small businesses in terms of ITSM is the level of investment in tools and technologies. Large enterprises often have the financial resources to invest in sophisticated ITSM software, which provides comprehensive features such as automation, reporting, and analytics. These tools help streamline processes, improve decision-making, and enhance service delivery by providing IT teams with valuable insights into performance. Small businesses, however, may not have the budget to invest in such advanced tools and often rely on more affordable or even free ITSM solutions that offer basic functionality. In many cases, small businesses may opt for simpler service management tools or even use existing productivity software, such as email and spreadsheets, to manage IT services. While these solutions may be adequate for smaller operations, they often lack the scalability and features necessary for more complex IT environments.

Another significant difference between large enterprises and small businesses in ITSM is the approach to resource allocation. Large enterprises typically have dedicated teams for each ITSM function, such as incident management, change management, and problem management. These teams work in a coordinated manner to ensure that IT services are delivered consistently and in line with business objectives. Small businesses, by contrast, often have smaller IT teams, and staff members are typically responsible for a wide range of tasks. IT professionals in small businesses often wear multiple hats, handling everything from service desk support to system administration, and may not have the same level of specialization as their counterparts in large enterprises. This lack of specialization can make it more difficult for small businesses to implement the full range of ITSM processes effectively, although it can also lead to a more flexible, dynamic approach to service management.

In summary, the role and implementation of ITSM in large enterprises and small businesses differ significantly due to differences in organizational size, resources, and complexity. Large enterprises benefit from formalized, structured ITSM frameworks that provide consistency, scalability, and control, while small businesses often rely on more flexible, responsive approaches that prioritize speed and cost-efficiency. Despite these differences, both types of organizations must ensure that their IT services are aligned with business goals, continuously improved, and capable of delivering value to users. Understanding these differences allows businesses to tailor their ITSM strategies to their specific needs and resources, ensuring that IT services are effectively managed and optimized for success.

ITSM for Outsourcing and Managed Services

As businesses increasingly rely on outsourcing and managed services to meet their IT needs, the role of IT Service Management (ITSM) becomes ever more critical in ensuring the delivery of high-quality, consistent, and reliable services. Outsourcing IT functions and leveraging managed services offer organizations the ability to reduce costs, access specialized expertise, and improve operational efficiency. However, these benefits come with unique challenges in managing service delivery, quality, and accountability. ITSM frameworks such as ITIL (Information Technology Infrastructure Library) play a crucial role in helping organizations navigate these challenges, ensuring that outsourced IT services align with business goals and meet the required service standards.

When outsourcing IT functions or engaging with managed service providers, organizations face a fundamental shift in how services are delivered and managed. Unlike traditional in-house IT operations, where the organization has direct control over the delivery of services, outsourcing and managed services often involve third-party providers who are responsible for the day-to-day management of IT resources. This shift necessitates a more structured approach to service management to ensure that the outsourced services meet organizational expectations and business needs. ITSM frameworks provide the structure and processes necessary to manage the relationship between the organization and its service providers, ensuring that services are delivered in a way that aligns with both operational and strategic objectives.

One of the key elements of ITSM for outsourcing and managed services is the establishment of clear and comprehensive service level agreements (SLAs). SLAs are formal agreements between the organization and the service provider that outline the specific expectations for service delivery, including performance metrics such as response times, resolution times, availability, and uptime. These agreements define the level of service the provider is obligated to deliver and provide a basis for monitoring and evaluating performance. ITSM frameworks, particularly those that emphasize service level management, help organizations establish SLAs that are realistic, measurable, and aligned with business priorities. In outsourced or managed service environments, SLAs serve as the foundation for managing performance, ensuring that the organization's IT needs are met in accordance with predefined standards.

In addition to SLAs, ITSM best practices emphasize the importance of continuous monitoring and performance management when outsourcing or using managed services. Organizations must implement processes to track the performance of outsourced IT services and ensure that they are consistently meeting agreed-upon service levels. This involves setting up monitoring tools and systems that provide real-time data on service performance, which can then be analyzed to identify any deviations from the SLAs. By incorporating ITSM processes such as incident management, problem management, and change management, organizations can ensure that issues with outsourced services are detected and addressed promptly. Regular performance reviews and audits also play a key role in ensuring that the service provider is meeting the terms of the agreement and delivering value to the business.

Effective communication between the organization and the managed service provider is essential for successful ITSM in outsourcing relationships. ITSM frameworks stress the importance of clear, transparent communication channels that allow both parties to address issues, provide feedback, and collaborate on improvements. Regular meetings, performance reviews, and status reports ensure that any concerns or opportunities for improvement are identified early, fostering a strong, productive relationship between the organization and its service provider. These communication processes also help prevent misunderstandings and ensure that both parties are aligned on expectations and objectives. A lack of effective communication can lead to service disruptions, missed SLAs, and overall dissatisfaction, making it a critical aspect of ITSM for outsourcing and managed services.

Another key aspect of ITSM for outsourcing and managed services is managing the integration between in-house IT operations and the third-party provider. In many cases, organizations continue to maintain some in-house IT functions while outsourcing others, creating a hybrid IT environment. ITSM frameworks help manage this complexity by providing processes and tools that ensure seamless integration between internal and external services. For example, incident management and service request fulfillment must be coordinated between in-house IT teams and external providers to ensure that service disruptions are resolved quickly and efficiently. Similarly, change management processes must account for both internal and external systems, ensuring that changes made by the service provider do not conflict with or disrupt in-house systems. Managing the integration of outsourced services with internal IT operations is essential for maintaining service continuity and minimizing risks.

Risk management is another critical area where ITSM plays a vital role in outsourcing and managed services. When organizations outsource critical IT functions, they are inherently exposed to risks related to data security, service disruptions, and compliance violations. ITSM frameworks provide a structured approach to identifying, assessing, and mitigating these risks. For example, in the case of cybersecurity risks, ITSM processes can be used to establish security protocols, ensure that the service provider adheres to industry security standards, and regularly audit the security posture of the outsourced services. ITSM also helps organizations manage compliance requirements by ensuring that both internal and external services meet the necessary regulatory standards, such as data privacy laws or industry-specific regulations. This proactive approach to risk management ensures that organizations can minimize the potential negative impact of outsourcing or managed services on their operations and reputation.

Another key consideration when using ITSM for outsourcing and managed services is ensuring that the service provider has the necessary resources, capabilities, and expertise to deliver the services effectively. It is not enough to simply sign a contract and rely on the provider to deliver; organizations must engage in due diligence to ensure that the provider has the necessary tools, infrastructure, and talent to meet the required service levels. ITSM processes such as vendor management and performance evaluation are crucial for assessing the provider's capabilities and ensuring that they continue to meet the organization's needs. Regular assessments and reviews help identify areas where the service provider may need additional support or where service improvements can be made.

ITSM frameworks also help organizations manage the ongoing optimization of outsourced services. Continuous improvement is a core principle of ITSM, and it is especially important in outsourcing relationships. As business needs change and technology evolves, organizations must ensure that their outsourced services remain aligned with these changes. ITSM processes such as service review, problem management, and service improvement planning provide a structured approach for identifying areas where outsourced services can be enhanced, whether by introducing new technologies, refining processes, or addressing recurring issues. By incorporating continuous improvement into the outsourcing relationship, organizations can ensure that they are getting the most value from their service providers and that services evolve to meet future business needs.

In conclusion, ITSM plays a crucial role in ensuring the success of outsourcing and managed services by providing a structured framework for managing service delivery, performance, risks, and integration. By applying ITSM best practices such as service level management, incident management, and continuous improvement, organizations can ensure that their outsourced services meet business needs, adhere to SLAs, and remain aligned with evolving technological and operational requirements. Effective communication, strong governance, and proactive risk management are essential for managing outsourced services, ensuring that service providers deliver value and contribute to the organization's overall success. As outsourcing and managed services continue to grow in importance, ITSM will remain a key enabler of successful service delivery, helping organizations manage their external relationships effectively and optimize their IT operations.

Case Studies of Successful ITSM Implementations

The successful implementation of IT Service Management (ITSM) can transform the way an organization manages its IT services, ensuring efficiency, alignment with business goals, and enhanced user satisfaction. Across industries, various organizations have leveraged ITSM frameworks like ITIL (Information Technology Infrastructure Library) to streamline processes, improve service delivery, and better manage service disruptions. Examining case studies of successful ITSM implementations can provide valuable insights into how organizations have navigated the complexities of service management and achieved substantial improvements in their IT operations.

One notable example of a successful ITSM implementation comes from a global telecommunications company that faced significant challenges in managing its vast IT infrastructure and services. Prior to implementing ITSM, the organization struggled with inconsistent service delivery, prolonged response times, and difficulty in tracking performance metrics across different regions. With a growing customer base and increasing demand for reliable services, the company recognized the need to adopt a more structured approach to IT service management. After adopting the ITIL framework, the organization implemented standardized processes for incident management, problem management, change management, and service request fulfillment.

By introducing ITIL's service desk model, the company was able to streamline its support processes, reducing response and resolution times for service incidents. Automation tools were introduced for incident logging, categorization, and prioritization, allowing support teams to quickly address high-priority issues. The organization also implemented robust performance monitoring and reporting systems, enabling IT teams to track key performance indicators (KPIs) and measure service delivery against established service level agreements (SLAs). Over time, the company experienced a significant reduction in downtime and a marked improvement in customer satisfaction. Additionally, the improved service delivery allowed the company to better align its IT services with its business goals, resulting in more efficient use of resources and higher profitability.

Another successful ITSM implementation can be found in the healthcare sector, where an organization adopted ITIL to improve its IT service management processes. The healthcare industry is highly regulated, with strict compliance and security requirements. The organization faced difficulties in managing patient data securely, ensuring the availability of critical medical applications, and meeting the demanding performance standards set by regulatory bodies. The decision to implement ITSM was driven by the need to ensure that IT services supported the organization's mission to provide high-quality healthcare while adhering to stringent regulatory requirements.

By implementing ITIL, the organization standardized its incident management process, ensuring that IT issues related to medical applications and systems were prioritized and resolved quickly. ITIL's problem management process was also introduced, allowing the IT team to identify recurring issues and root causes more effectively, leading to long-term fixes and better system reliability. Change management processes were put in place to ensure that changes to critical healthcare applications and infrastructure were carefully assessed, tested, and implemented with minimal risk to patient care services. Additionally, the organization introduced ITIL's service level management practices to track and manage SLAs, ensuring that IT services were delivered within agreed-upon performance standards. As a result, the organization was able to significantly reduce service disruptions, improve system reliability, and maintain compliance with regulatory requirements, all while enhancing the overall user experience for healthcare providers and patients.

In the financial services sector, another organization turned to ITSM to address the challenges of managing IT services across a complex, distributed environment. The company, which provided a wide range of financial products, faced significant issues with service consistency, communication breakdowns, and a lack of visibility into IT operations. To address these challenges, the company adopted ITIL to streamline its service management processes and improve coordination across departments. The implementation was focused on standardizing IT service delivery, improving collaboration between IT teams, and enhancing customer satisfaction.

The company began by implementing a centralized service desk and introducing a comprehensive incident management system. This allowed the organization to provide a single point of contact for all IT-related issues, ensuring that service disruptions were addressed quickly and effectively. Additionally, the company adopted ITIL's change management processes to ensure that IT changes were handled in a controlled manner, minimizing the impact on critical business operations. Over time, the organization was able to improve communication between IT and business teams, aligning IT services with business goals more effectively. The introduction of performance tracking tools and regular service reviews allowed the company to continually assess and improve its IT service management practices, resulting in a more agile IT environment that could better respond to changing business needs. The successful implementation of ITSM led to higher operational efficiency, reduced costs, and improved customer satisfaction, helping the company maintain a competitive edge in the financial services industry.

Another example comes from a large retail chain that sought to optimize its IT services to support the expansion of its online and in-store operations. With a growing customer base and increasing demand for real-time data and services, the company faced challenges in ensuring the availability and reliability of its IT systems. The organization adopted the ITIL framework to implement standardized processes across its IT service management functions and to improve the overall service delivery model.

The company's ITSM implementation focused on incident and problem management to ensure that issues with its e-commerce platform, point-of-sale systems, and back-office applications were quickly addressed. ITIL's service desk model was used to centralize support operations, enabling the IT team to handle incidents efficiently and provide timely resolutions. Additionally, the company adopted ITIL's capacity management and performance monitoring processes to ensure that its IT infrastructure could scale to meet the growing demand from both online and in-store customers. Through the introduction of continuous service improvement processes, the company was able to assess its service delivery on an ongoing basis, identify areas for optimization, and make data-driven decisions to improve the quality of IT services. As a result, the retail chain saw improved system uptime, reduced customer complaints, and enhanced the overall shopping experience for its customers, both online and in-store.

A key takeaway from these case studies is that the successful implementation of ITSM in diverse industries shares several common factors. One of the most important elements is the alignment of IT services with the broader business objectives. Whether in telecommunications, healthcare, financial services, or retail, organizations that successfully implement ITSM frameworks understand that IT is not just a technical function but a strategic enabler of business success. By ensuring that IT services are aligned with business needs and customer expectations, organizations can create more efficient, reliable, and customer-focused IT environments.

Additionally, effective communication and collaboration between IT and business units are essential for ensuring that ITSM processes are integrated into everyday operations. Organizations that prioritize cross-functional collaboration and involve business leaders in the ITSM process are more likely to see success in their IT service management initiatives. Furthermore, the use of performance metrics, regular reviews, and continuous improvement practices is critical for ensuring that IT services remain aligned with evolving business needs and that service quality improves over time.

In all of these cases, the implementation of ITSM has led to improved service delivery, reduced downtime, better alignment of IT services with business goals, and enhanced customer satisfaction. These examples demonstrate that no matter the size, industry, or complexity of the organization, ITSM frameworks provide valuable tools for managing and optimizing IT services, ultimately supporting the organization's long-term success.

The Path Forward: Developing a Comprehensive ITSM Strategy

As businesses face an increasingly complex and dynamic technological landscape, the need for a well-defined and comprehensive IT Service Management (ITSM) strategy becomes more crucial than ever. The adoption of ITSM frameworks like ITIL (Information Technology Infrastructure Library) has proven to be an effective way to streamline IT processes, enhance service delivery, and align IT operations with business goals. However, developing a robust ITSM strategy is not a one-size-fits-all approach. It requires careful planning, collaboration across departments, and a deep understanding of both current IT needs and future business objectives. The path forward for any organization seeking to implement or enhance its ITSM strategy involves several key stages, including assessing current practices, defining goals, aligning IT with business, and continuously evolving ITSM processes.

The first step in developing a comprehensive ITSM strategy is conducting a thorough assessment of the current state of IT services within the organization. This involves evaluating existing IT processes, tools, and resources to identify gaps, inefficiencies, or areas where service delivery could be improved. For many organizations, the journey toward ITSM begins with a recognition that their current IT management approach is no longer sufficient to meet growing demands or evolving business needs. A comprehensive assessment can reveal areas such as poor incident resolution times, ineffective change management practices, or inadequate service level monitoring. Understanding these pain points allows the organization to prioritize which areas of ITSM need the most attention and resources. Additionally, this assessment should involve gathering input from various stakeholders, including IT staff, business leaders, and end-users, to gain a holistic view of the challenges and opportunities in IT service management.

Once the current state has been assessed, the next step is to define clear and measurable goals for the ITSM strategy. These goals should align with the overall business objectives and should focus on improving both the efficiency of IT operations and the quality of service delivery. For instance, one goal may be to reduce service downtime by improving incident response times or implementing proactive problem management processes. Another goal could be to enhance the user experience by streamlining service requests or improving the accuracy and speed of IT support. It is important that these goals are specific, measurable, achievable, relevant, and time-bound (SMART), as this provides a clear roadmap for success and allows for tracking progress over time. In addition to IT-specific goals, the ITSM strategy should aim to align IT services with business objectives. This ensures that IT is not working in isolation but is actively contributing to the organization's broader strategic goals.

Aligning IT with business objectives is one of the most critical aspects of developing an effective ITSM strategy. Many organizations struggle with the disconnect between IT operations and business needs. IT departments may focus on technical excellence, while business leaders may prioritize speed, cost-effectiveness, and customer experience. A comprehensive ITSM strategy ensures that IT services are designed, delivered, and measured with business priorities in mind. For example, if the business strategy focuses on expanding digital services, the ITSM strategy should prioritize the availability and reliability of digital platforms and the seamless integration of new technologies. Collaboration between IT and business units is essential to ensure that IT services are aligned with and support the company's mission, customer experience goals, and growth initiatives. This alignment allows IT teams to better understand the impact of their services on business outcomes and ensures that IT resources are focused on high-priority initiatives.

The next critical step in developing an ITSM strategy is the adoption of best practices and frameworks. ITIL, the most widely adopted ITSM framework, provides a structured approach to managing IT services and improving service delivery. ITIL emphasizes the importance of standardized processes for key areas such as incident management, change management, problem management, service desk operations, and service level management. By leveraging ITIL best practices, organizations can establish clear guidelines for managing IT services, reduce operational inefficiencies, and ensure consistency in service delivery. However, organizations must recognize that ITIL and other ITSM frameworks should not be adopted blindly. The strategy should take into account the specific needs, culture, and scale of the organization. In some cases, organizations may need to tailor ITIL processes to fit their unique environment or to integrate ITSM with other frameworks such as Agile or DevOps.

Technology plays a significant role in the development of an ITSM strategy. Choosing the right tools and technologies is essential for automating processes, improving service delivery, and enhancing overall IT service management. ITSM tools are designed to streamline service management processes, such as incident tracking, service request fulfillment, change management, and performance monitoring. These tools allow organizations to automate routine tasks, capture real-time data on service performance, and provide IT teams with valuable insights into how services are being delivered. When selecting ITSM tools, it is important to consider factors such as scalability, ease of integration with existing systems, user experience, and customization options. Organizations should also evaluate whether cloud-based or on-premise solutions are more appropriate, depending on their specific needs. A well-chosen ITSM tool can significantly improve efficiency, reduce manual workloads, and provide greater visibility into service performance.

Implementing an ITSM strategy requires effective change management. The introduction of new ITSM processes, tools, or practices can often be met with resistance, particularly if employees are accustomed to existing workflows. To ensure successful adoption, organizations must foster a culture of change readiness. This includes providing adequate training and resources for IT staff, communicating the benefits of ITSM to all stakeholders, and ensuring that IT and business teams collaborate throughout the implementation process. Change management should be treated as an ongoing process rather than a one-time event. This involves regularly reviewing ITSM practices to ensure they remain relevant and responsive to business needs and evolving technology trends.

Once the strategy has been implemented, continuous improvement is essential to ensure that ITSM processes remain effective and aligned with organizational goals. ITSM is not a static set of practices; it must evolve over time to address new challenges and capitalize on emerging technologies. By regularly measuring key performance indicators

(KPIs), collecting feedback from end-users, and conducting performance reviews, organizations can identify areas where their ITSM strategy needs to be adjusted or enhanced. Continuous improvement should be embedded in the ITSM culture, encouraging teams to find innovative solutions, refine processes, and adapt to changes in the business or technological landscape.

As organizations move forward with their ITSM strategy, they must also consider scalability. The ITSM strategy should be flexible enough to adapt to future growth, changes in business priorities, or new technological advancements. Whether the organization is expanding into new markets, adopting cloud technologies, or transitioning to an Agile development model, the ITSM strategy must be able to support these changes. Scalability ensures that the ITSM framework can continue to deliver value even as the organization evolves.

The development of a comprehensive ITSM strategy is an ongoing journey, not a one-time effort. It requires a clear understanding of the current IT environment, alignment with business goals, and a commitment to continuous improvement. By following a structured approach, engaging stakeholders, adopting best practices, and leveraging technology, organizations can build an ITSM strategy that not only meets current demands but is also capable of adapting to future challenges. With the right strategy in place, IT can become a key enabler of business success, driving efficiency, improving customer experiences, and supporting the organization's long-term goals.